God Whispers

Are

Life Changers

Transforming Life Lessons through a
True-Life Adventure

MICHAEL SALKELD

God Whispers Are Life Changers

Trilogy Christian Publishers
A Wholly Owned Subsidiary of Trinity Broadcasting Network
2442 Michelle Drive, Tustin, CA 92780

10 9 8 7 6 5 4 3 2 1
Library of Congress Cataloging-in-Publication Data is available.

ISBN: 979-8-89597-086-7
E-ISBN: 979-8-89597-087-4

PRAISE FOR
God Whispers Are Life Changers

God whispers and we listen. Or do we? This book is filled with many captivating vignettes of a faith-filled couple who heard the whispers of God—and listened. The adventure that ensued is one for the ages! This book will encourage you to learn to listen to His whispers yourself and find your own adventure. You will get to the end and say, "Only God."

— Jamie Rasmussen,
senior pastor, Scottsdale Bible Church,
author of *How Joyful People Think*
and *When God Feels Far Away*

...but the LORD was not in the wind. And after the wind an earthquake, but the LORD was not in the earthquake. And after the earthquake a fire, but the LORD was not in the fire. And after the fire the sound of a low whisper. And when Elijah heard it, he wrapped his face in his cloak and went out and stood at the entrance of the cave. And behold, there came a voice to him...

—1 Kings 19:11–13 ESV

DEDICATION

To my mom, Mae Salkeld, who gave me a heart for the less fortunate, and whose most memorable saying from my childhood years was, "There but for the grace of God go I!"

and

To my wife, Delane, who inspired me and walked hand in hand with me every day of this adventure.

and

To my mother-in-law, Barbara LaRue, who introduced me to the writings of Dr. Robert H. Schuller, which had such a profound influence on my life.

CONTENTS

ACKNOWLEDGMENTS

Special acknowledgment and appreciation goes to the following organizations and individuals who work tirelessly, day after day, in the ministries and churches included in the stories in this book, and to my church pastors, who, for the past thirty-five years, have provided inspiration and instruction through their God-led teaching, as well as their encouragement to serve the underprivileged and disadvantaged in our community and across the globe.

Our thanks and hearts go out to each of them.

Organizations

- *Hour of Power*
- Christian Relief Services, Inc.
- Bread and Water for Africa
- Mentor Kids, USA
- Bridge-2-Hope

Individuals

- Pastor Bobby Schuller
- Bryan Krizek, Christian Relief Services, Inc.
- Bethelhem Tessema, Bread and Water for Africa
- Angela Miyanda, Kabwata Orphanage and Transit Centre
- Aaron Parrott, Mentor Kids, USA
- Nora Espinoza, Mentor Kids, USA
- Alejandra Arellano, Mentor Kids, USA
- Mary Jane Utterback, Mentor Kids, USA

- Wendy Mahoney, Northeast Phoenix Neighborhood Action Alliance
- Amy Seiser, Bridge-2-Hope
- Senior Pastor Jamie Rasmussen, Scottsdale Bible Church
- Pastor-Emeritus Dr. Darryl DelHousaye, Scottsdale Bible Church
- Pastor Ryan Heath, Scottsdale Bible Church, Northridge Campus
- Pastor Martin Gonzalez, Vida En Cristo AZ
- Pastor Macario De la Cruz, Rivers Church
- Shannon Mitchell, Scottsdale Bible Church

With special thanks to Pastor Bobby Schuller and Hour of Power for allowing us to reprint his devotional *The Power in Hearing Hearts*, found in Postscript II.

And my apologies to anyone else whom I have failed to mention here.

The author's royalties from sales of this book will be used to continue supporting the God-led charities and ministries described in these stories.

INTRODUCTION

A baby boy was born in 2017 to a teenage mom who soon abandoned him in Lusaka, the capital city of Zambia, and he became one of the more than 1.2 million orphans under the age of fifteen in that south-central African country. He was born deaf, and initially was thought to be unable to speak. He was taken to Kabwata Orphanage (named after a neighborhood in Lusaka, Zambia) as an infant and would join the fifty-plus children already living there, who would become his "brothers and sisters."

Angela was their "mother" at the orphanage that she had founded almost twenty years before, and they would have many "aunties," women who dedicated their lives to loving and nurturing the children, helping to raise them and give them a future that most orphans in Zambia could only dream about. We were told that without Kabwata, Angela, and others, the baby boy would have had little chance of surviving infancy in this sub-Saharan country where the infant death rate is five times the rate in the United States, and if he had, he "likely would have been used to beg on the streets for his livelihood."

Six years later, however, he was working hard, making progress each and every day in overcoming the challenges posed by his lack of hearing and speech. Angela once said he was one of the most intelligent toddlers she'd ever met. Following a medical assessment, it was confirmed that he would need to attend a special school in Lusaka for hard-of-hearing children, where he is now enrolled and thriving. Now a talented young student, he has been learning to speak using sign language.

His name is "Michael," and Michael is a true blessing from God to the world, to Kabwata Orphanage, to his "brothers," "sisters," "aunties," and Angela, and especially to us, my wife, Delane, and me. In Zambia, it is tradition that a village elder should name a new baby, and that's how we came to know Michael.

My wife, Delane and I had been helping to support Kabwata Orphanage for ten years, and we were on our second visit to visit Angela and the kids in 2017, the year Michael was born. Much to our surprise, Angela asked us to name the new baby, the new member of the Kabwata family.

We were so deeply honored, and after much consideration, we chose the name Michael—after the great archangel of the Bible. Michael, the archangel, was a spiritual warrior in the battle of good and evil, a champion of justice. Our prayer was that the strength of this namesake would be a blessing upon little Michael, who had started life without much hope, but through the grace of God was given a home, a family, and a future. *Michael* was, indeed, a fitting name, and Michael was, indeed, a blessing from God!

Kabwata Orphanage is just one of the many ministries and adventures—including founding and growing our company, ParaWest—that God has led us to through His *whispers* over the past twenty years. The ministries we've been blessed to serve, both financially and with the sweat of our brow, have been such an integral part of our adventure that it seemed appropriate to begin this book here.

In his very successful book series that share "God Winks," Squire Bushnell talks about seeming coincidences that occur, which, when looked at closer or looked back upon, are clearly God's doing. I like to call them "God *whispers*," but these God *whispers* are somewhat different. They're *whispers* you hear in your heart. They're *whispers* that provide both guidance and confirmation along your path in life. I believe every Christian experiences them, but the choice to act upon them or to ignore them is a decision each individual must make of their own "free will."

Over the past twenty years, Delane and I have been blessed to have heard and acted on His *whispers*, and it's safe to say that there have been too many to count. But through these many years, those *whispers* have been as clear to us as if He'd written a script for our lives and revealed it along the way.

Today, ParaWest Management, our apartment management company (named to complement our former partner's name, "Para-mount Financial"), has offices in Scottsdale, Arizona, and Houston, Texas, and operates in more than fifteen cities across five states. Over the past twenty years, we've managed real estate assets valued at more than $1.5 billion and completed renovation projects totaling more than $75 million. All this takes a big team, and we have nearly two hundred employees to get the job done. That "job" is to provide desirable, high-quality rental housing to our residents, as well as investment management services to our clients and partners.

Although the means that ParaWest has provided toward ministries may not be considered "substantial" in a world where new mega-millionaires and -billionaires are minted each year due to the global reach of the internet, we have been blessed to be able to use the resources that He has given us in ways that have impacted and changed many lives along the way. And we have seen how He can take any means or gift, no matter how large or small, and multiply its effect many times over in doing good in this world!

Initially, this book was going to just be a self-improvement-type guide about our adventure and God's hand in it, with self-help suggestions to the reader along the way to provide ideas on how to look to similar possibilities in their own life. It seems like every book today lays out some kind of "action steps" (e.g., step 1, 2, 3...) to achieve something, and that was to be the initial premise. After much reflection, however, we determined that God didn't want us to share just a "1, 2, 3 to-do list." He wanted us to tell *our story*, to encourage readers from their own perspective and their own circumstances to look to Him for inspiration, direction, discernment, and wisdom... to listen for His *whispers* in their own lives.

So, that's what we've done. This is our story, our lives, our legacy. It's a legacy of business, ministries, people, places, and faith, all driven by His *whispers*. It's a legacy that includes our entrepreneurial adventure with God, a story about starting and growing a business that we had never planned to start, woven with stories of the ministries we had never planned to serve, and God's hand in all of it and in the lives that have been touched along the way.

Our adventure has been about looking to Him for guidance and thanking Him each and every day. It's about working hard and smart, doing the best we can and applying strong values and principles, so that we're positioned for Him to use us for His glory. And it's about using the God-given resources He has provided to help others along the way, to be His light in this world, as well as His hands and His feet. We know we could never have accomplished these things on our own. It has been God's doing and God's plan all along!

In the following pages, we'll take you on our adventure with God at our side. Yes, it's been a true adventure, taking us from Scottsdale, Arizona, to Houston, Texas, and halfway around the world to Africa. Our journey has impacted thousands of lives, including our own employees, partners, and clients, and those we've served, including underprivileged children and families, homeless families, refugees, orphaned children, and many others. We'll describe the successes and the failures, the good times and the struggles, and how we've seen God's hand in it all along the way.

And yet, even though this story is about our lives, our business, and our adventure, it could easily be rewritten to tell the story of almost anyone, in any job or any business. We believe that no matter where you're at in life, you can fulfill your dreams by listening to God's *whispers*, working hard, and seeking and following His will. Our prayer for you, dear reader, is that you'll listen to your own God *whispers* and find your passion and self-fulfillment through a God-led adventure that will bring you all that your heart desires—as you look to Him and seek to help others along the way.

"God Notes"

In writing this book, we found that there were so many great stories of how God had worked in our lives; however, many of them didn't fit directly into the narrative of our entrepreneurial adventure. So, we've included them along the way and called them "God Notes" (i.e., footnotes from God). Hopefully, some of these may invoke readers' stories of their own.

PROLOGUE

So, there we were, nine of us including our Zambian guide, riding barely two feet out of the water in a narrow, twenty-foot aluminum skiff powered by a lightweight, thirty-five-horsepower outboard motor. The year was 2023, and we were on a river safari on the Lower Zambezi River, gliding along the water between Zambia and Zimbabwe on a cool winter (in Africa) July day looking for wildlife.

We had seen some already. We had come across a pod of hippos milling about in the water not far down the shoreline from our skiff, and for the moment, we were idling in the river just over ten feet from the sandy shoreline, on which the biggest, scariest-looking Nile crocodile we could imagine was sunning himself.

Surely, he was the granddaddy of the river, a monster at least twenty feet long and huge around the girth. His head alone had to have been three feet in length, and those giant, clenched jaws made of massive muscle were protruding outward to the sides. As we approached the shore, our guide pointed out that Nile crocodiles are the largest of the species in the world, and the most ferocious, with sixty-eight razor-sharp, cone-shaped teeth, and a jaw that could come together with more than five thousand pounds per square inch of bone-snapping pressure on whatever prey he might choose to annihilate. His eyes were closed, he was still as a ghost, and he appeared to be quite complacent while enjoying the sunshine.

But all that changed in a heartbeat. While we were snapping photos and enjoying our photographic subject, his steely-gray eyes blinked wide, his massive jaws opened, and he let out a low, guttural roar that shook us to the bone. In an instant, his entire front end, including those massive jaws, made a 90-degree pivot in our direction as he slapped his head hard upon the water, generating a "smacking" sound, and lunged into the water toward us.

We were petrified. Our thirteen-year-old granddaughter shrieked, we all gasped, and for a moment, time stood still. Then, while the monster was still submerged beneath the murky river water, time started back up, our guide gunned that little thirty-horsepower motor, and we skittered away, collectively catching our breath. In our haste, however, we had motored toward the hippo pod, and within seconds, we were gunning the engine even harder to make it past them before one of those two-ton monsters reared its giant head, bared its six-inch incisors, and capsized our little boat.

And that was just the beginning, because as soon as we made it safely past those immense hippopotami, we rounded a large bend in the river, and that's when we saw them, standing before us in all their glory: majestic African elephants, the largest land mammals on earth.

They ranged in height from eight to twelve feet tall, with their gigantic, floppy, oversized ears; dirty gray coats; long, narrow trunks pulling up clumps of grass and feeding it into their mouths; and tails swishing behind, flicking off flies as they ate. We were looking at a small herd of these glorious creatures along the riverbank feasting on the dry grasses. They were led by a massive bull nearly twelve feet tall, with enormous eight-foot tusks, flanked by younger males with smaller tusks, and females.

There were ten—no, twelve—no, fifteen—of these stately animals just fifty feet from our little boat. It was truly a sight to behold, and we were "amazed," "astonished," "exhilarated," and "thankful"… for the incredible opportunity of seeing these majestic creatures in the wild! Yes, it was an exhilarating boat ride to say the least, and we had just arrived at our safari lodge on the river an hour earlier. What a start to our Zambezi adventure!

This was our third trip to Zambia in central Africa, and it was our first safari on this remote part of the Lower Zambezi River located about a hundred miles southeast of Lusaka, the capital city of Zambia. The safari was a brief diversion from our primary purpose for being there, which was to spend time at an orphanage in Lusaka with which Delane and I had been working for the past sixteen years. We had worked with the orphanage as an outreach ministry and had been able to help support this and other international and domestic ministries through the "sweat of our brow," combined with financial resources generated by our company, "ParaWest," which we had founded on a shoestring budget some twenty-plus years prior.

Delane and I had brought our adult son Chris; his thirteen-year-old daughter (our granddaughter), Haylee; and our fourteen-year-old adopted daughter, Roslyn, with us on this trip. We wanted them to meet the kids at the orphanage and begin their own relationships, and to better understand the efforts and impact of our African ministries firsthand. The river safari had been tacked on as a bonus, to enable them to experience the extraordinary wonders of this great continent for themselves. Yes, Africa was a part of our legacy, and we wanted them to understand it and embrace it, and to continue it into the future, and that was why we were there.

PART I
In the Beginning

NAVAJO NATION

HOUSTON

SCOTTSDALE

God Whispers Are Life Changers

CHAPTER 1

Downsized

We hadn't planned on starting our own business, and we certainly hadn't planned the adventure it would lead us on for the next twenty-plus years of our lives. We both had successful careers and were not considering the risks and dramatic life changes that starting a business would entail. If we've learned anything in this life, however, it's that we're not in total control, and the paths we're led down may be far different from those of our early hopes, dreams, and aspirations. So we began our adventure in March 2003, and here's what led up to that.

It was President's Day, February 17, 2003, but I had to work. The company I had worked with for the past six months was quite small, and the owner didn't accommodate many holidays other than the biggies such as Christmas, the Fourth of July, Thanksgiving, and the like. Delane was staying home that day as her company did, in fact, celebrate the holiday.

Our workday started early, so I arrived at the office at 7:30 a.m. As I walked into the office that day, however, things were different. My boss had moved into what had been our controller's office the previous Friday, and no one else was around. So I stepped into his office to chat, and over the next five minutes, I learned he was "downsizing" the company—including my job, which no longer existed. And, as they say, that was that. Out the door I went, with a modicum of severance and vacation pay, not the way I had expected to start my week.

When I arrived back home a little after eight, Delane was just getting out of bed. Somewhat still in shock, I rambled on to her about what had happened, and of course, she, too, was taken aback. We hadn't seen this coming. Losing my job, however, was only the half of it. Delane had been notified about a week earlier that the company she was working for was *also* downsizing, and her salary was being cut in half. We hadn't seen that one coming, either, but at that time, we felt that as long as I was working, we'd be okay. But not anymore!

Now, anyone who's been working for a few years is familiar with that ugly term: *downsized*. It's kind of a wannabe respectful explanation for firing people: "laying them off." However, the truth is, it's a terribly negative term, and its effects, although often inadvertent, hurt people's lives. Livelihoods are important. It's how we pay the bills, put food on the table, and keep a roof overhead. It also gives us meaning and purpose, or at least adds to it. So, yes, *downsized* is not a positive word in any sense, but it is one so many must deal with at some point in their lives.

Anyone who's ever lost a job, either through cutbacks, layoffs, or for any other reason, understands the emotions and insecurities that grab you. Thoughts go through your mind like, *What am I going to do? How will we support our family? How will this affect our teenage boys, and how will we ever be able to send them to college? Will I ever be able to get another job?* and on and on and on. We had nowhere to turn. We had no fallback plan.

So we looked to the Lord for guidance, and we heard His *whispers*, and shortly thereafter, we had our direction and the start of a plan.

Delane and I had worked in the same profession—the apartment investment and management industry—and each of us had cultivated successful careers dating back more than two decades. We had worked together for several years a while back before going different directions with different employers. We knew we worked well together, and we knew each other's strengths and abilities.

We had occasionally broached the idea of starting our own company, but we'd never gotten serious, as the financial startup funding had been beyond our reach and the risk of not having a paycheck was too great. This time was different, however. This time we were hearing God's *whisper* that we should "step out in faith," and this time God provided a simple starting point and a plan for action. God's *whisper* was strong, indeed!

So we decided to step out in faith and go for it. We prayed for guidance and began developing the plan He had placed in our hearts. Within three weeks, we had our first clients and were open for business. What we didn't know at the time, however, was that this was the beginning of a lifelong adventure. God knew, though, as this had been His plan for our adventure all along!

GOD NOTE
God's Sense of Humor

Ever since the day I met Delane, she's talked about God's sense of humor. She says He indeed has a sense of humor and expresses it in so many ways in each of our lives.

Well before we started ParaWest, God had known that Delane and I were unhappy in our jobs. She had an unappreciative boss, and I had one who expected me to arrive before office hours on Monday so we could have a staff meeting on our "own time," before actually "starting" our workweek, and on top of that, we were not to expect holidays off except for Christmas, Thanksgiving, the Fourth of July, and a few of the other "biggies."

So, He decided to fix that for us, and He blessed us with ParaWest, and we, in turn, responded in one of our earliest personnel policy decisions. With only five employees on our three apartment properties to start (of course, we couldn't have known that twenty years down the road, we'd have nearly two hundred employees), we started developing policies and compiling our employee manual.

We wanted to make sure our employees would enjoy their work and feel more appreciated than we had been, so early on, we decided to offer an extensive holiday listing for our employees to be able to enjoy time off with their families and loved ones. We started with President's Day, then included just about every holiday we could think of and some that weren't even holidays, such as the days after Thanksgiving and Christmas. As new holidays are proclaimed, we add them to our approved list. Now, some twenty years later, our employees are still enjoying those early decisions, and we're quite certain God must have smiled at that!

CHAPTER 2

On a Wing and a Prayer

Many successful companies have started with next to nothing and succeeded beyond their founder's wildest imaginations.

- In 1971, Starbucks was started by two teachers and a writer who pooled their money to start their Seattle-based coffee bean business. The concept of Starbucks as a coffee shop didn't come about until 1982, and the rest is history.[1]
- Founded in 1965 with just a thousand dollars borrowed from a family friend, Subway started as "Peter's Super Submarines," a small sandwich shop in Bridgeport, Connecticut, and now it operates in more than one hundred countries.
- Hewlett-Packard began in 1939 with an investment of $538, and through the years, it expanded into all sorts of electronics before making its foray into computers in 1968. Today the company is worth more than $63 billion.[2]

Our own business, ParaWest, truly started on "a wing and a prayer." We had minimal financial resources, no customers on day one, and no jobs to fall back on, so in short, we were on about the shortest shoestring budget imaginable. So, on our "wing and a prayer," and with a little faith, we started anyway, and here's what led up to that.

In order to provide the reader with some context as to the shoe-string budget we started with, and the simplistic plan we had, we'd like to provide a little background. When I was "downsized," I walked away with severance and vacation pay totaling a few thousand dollars. Delane was resigning from her job, so she had no severance. We had no savings, but we had started the process of refinancing our mortgage as our home's value had increased, and shortly thereafter, we were able to pull out another few thousand dollars to add to our startup funds. So we had our modest "nest egg" to begin with.

Although we had no clients, we decided we could approach three apartment property owners with whom Delane was working, as her company would no longer be servicing these clients with her leaving. With their downsizing, Delane's former employer would be focusing on their development business (i.e., building apartments instead of operating them). So we had enough to pay the bills for a few months, and we had three potential clients to pursue. If we could land these clients, we'd have enough income when combined with our nest egg to support us for the first several months, as long as we kept business expenses to a minimum.

Now, I had long wanted to be self-employed, "my own boss," ever since I'd started my career in my early twenties. God, however, had a different plan. As I later realized after we started ParaWest, it took all the experience and knowledge gained in all those prior years to start and grow a successful business. The same realization applied to Delane, at least with regard to her experience and knowledge. When it came to the part about wanting to be self-employed, she actually felt the opposite. She believed the responsibilities and time require-ments of being self-employed would place burdens on our lives that she didn't want.

So God met us in the middle. After allowing us to gain all the experience we needed through prior positions and more than twenty years' experience, He blessed us with ParaWest. Not only did it satisfy my longing to be self-employed, but it went far beyond alleviating Delane's concerns about having our personal and family lives encroached upon by an overly demanding business. ParaWest has given us more freedom than we ever could have imagined to pursue so many of the other directions and experiences that have enhanced our lives, from serving others, to travel, and not least of all, time to ourselves. He chose the time, the place, and the resources, and then He led the results to bless our lives in our entrepreneurial adventure through ParaWest.

The first step in our simplistic plan was to develop and print a company brochure to use as a presentation piece when meeting with our three potential clients to try to secure their business. With today's computer programs (even back in 2003), with only a weekend's worth of work, we were able to turn out a professional-quality full-color brochure/résumé touting all our previous experience as well as the services our company would provide.

To enhance the perception of our professionalism for our presentation, we had rented an address at a mailbox company nearby and used it in our materials to sound like we had an office address. We were actually working out of our home, with Delane having turned the guest room into her office and me setting up in the living room with two six-foot folding tables and a copier/printer, surrounded by boxes for files and materials. Our living room was no longer "livable," but we didn't expect to be doing much entertaining for a while anyway (but more on that later).

So, with a little enhanced presentation and creativity, and a strong hand from God, we were successful in landing the three clients. Our entrepreneurial endeavor, ParaWest, was off the ground.

CHAPTER 3

Homelessness and God's Hand

For the past twenty years, Michelle has lived a God-led life. She's had a wonderful job for many years, raised her three sons to adulthood, and seen them embark on their own careers. For the past fifteen years, she has served homeless families through a program called Bridge to Hope (B2H), in Phoenix, Arizona, but twenty years ago, Michelle was homeless herself. Yes, God has truly blessed her life and that of her children over these many years, and here's what led up to that.

Michelle was a single mom with three boys, ages three, eight, and nine, in 2004, when she fled her abusive husband with nothing but her three children and the clothes on their backs. She fled because she feared for her life, and she left in the middle of a physical fight with her husband, which was the last straw. A friend called a domestic violence shelter on Michelle's behalf, and that's where she went—and where the four of them would live for the next four months. It was a terrible time in their lives, and Michelle found herself in despair, with her boys "crying themselves to sleep each night," as she recounted years later.

One day a staff member at the shelter suggested that she might want to apply to a "faith-based program" called "The Bridge," later to be renamed "Bridge to Hope." And so she did. Her application was accepted, and that's where she would live for the next two years in a secure, loving, and learning environment, surrounded by her "church family." The Bridge was led by Amy Sue, who ran the program with all the love and dedication that only comes from a God-centered life. The program provided Michelle with a furnished two-bedroom apartment with bunk beds for the boys, and for Michelle, it was truly heaven on earth!

The Bridge took in homeless, single moms with their children, and provided all the necessities for living: a home, food, medical care, as well as the means to start a new life, vocational training, life skills training, and most importantly, a godly environment, including a "church team family" for each Bridge family. This church team family furnished their apartment, provided transportation as needed, celebrated holidays and special times together, and in short, did everything an extended family might do for their own family members. Delane and I became a part of Michelle's church family, with our church agreeing to pay the monthly support stipend. So, for the next two years, we spent time with Michelle and her sons, Daniel, Nathan, and Bazil, having fun, sharing holidays, celebrating life events, attending church, and just loving on them.

For a year and a half during that time, I'd pick up the three boys, and another two from the Bridge apartments, and take them to one of our family member churches that had an active kids' program on Wednesday evenings, where they'd participate in Bible study, games, and crafts. I would then pick them up when it ended at eight, and take them for burgers or pizza and then home. We had to trade in our Chrysler sedan for an SUV when we committed to taking on this task, but it was worth every penny as these boys thrived in the God-led Wednesday-night program!

At this point, we had been very blessed in starting our new company, and we wanted to share His blessings with those less fortunate. It was early in the life of our new business however, and we didn't have much in the way of funds to contribute, but God led us to be His "hands and feet" on this adventure instead—what a blessing!

Now fast-forward some eighteen years later. We received an invitation from Amy Sue at the renamed B2H to speak at their upcoming Thanksgiving dinner and share memories of our time with Michelle and the boys. Along with the invitation, Amy Sue provided us with an update on Michelle and her family, and here's what we learned. Michelle's life turned around entirely following her time at The Bridge. She had been employed for the previous fifteen years with the county judicial court system, where she had found employment through referrals and assistance from Bridge staff and volunteers while at The Bridge. She had purchased her own home, where she had raised her boys through young adulthood—and what a job raising them she had done! Daniel was now a proud U.S. Marine serving his country. Nathan was a youth pastor at a local church, and Bazil, the youngest, was in college pursing a degree.

Who would have ever imagined an outcome like this back in those early days, when Michelle was struggling, and we came alongside her just to try to help give her a new start. We couldn't have imagined it, but God did—it had been His plan all along!

CHAPTER 4

Declined

Off the ground we were. Fledgling entrepreneurs! Over the first few months, we landed a couple more clients and started growing. Delane and I worked well together with her overseeing property operations, me doing the accounting and "back office" stuff, and the two of us working together to seek out and secure new clients. It was a hectic time, but we were blessed, and we were loving it!

Then, just as we thought we were on our way and we started to expand, the "other shoe dropped." Our application to lease a small first office space for our fledgling company was declined! Much to our astonishment and dismay, we were turned down as a leasing candidate because our credit rating was too low. Wow! What a blow!

Now, as anyone knows who has ever been denied credit, whether for a credit card, a car loan, a home loan, or to lease an office, it's a jolt to your pride as well as to your overall self-confidence. My immediate thought was, *Maybe we won't even be able to lease an office for this fledgling new business of ours.* It was devastating. It was our first setback, and here's what led up to that.

As we took on additional clients by mid-2003, our home workspace got more and more cluttered with files, reports, presentation materials, etc., so by early summer, our living room was a disaster as far as functioning as a normal "living room" should. Now, as a man, I really didn't think much about it, but Delane clearly thought otherwise. So, when I suggested that we take one of the other bedrooms and turn it into another office (our sons were starting college and living on their own), Delane subtlety suggested that maybe we'd be better off finding office space to lease elsewhere. And so we did.

In 2003, it was not possible to search all available spaces on the internet, so I began driving around the area looking for leasing signs on office buildings. We wanted something close to home, but we were hampered by our very limited budget. We basically could afford to rent only about as much space as a small two-bedroom apartment, about 1,000 square feet, and larger office buildings don't often accommodate this small size.

After driving around the area for a few days, however, I finally found a small office suite in a "garden office building" not too far from our home. Typical of a garden office building, it had small suites with businesses surrounding a central, landscaped courtyard. Most real estate professionals would consider this a "Class C" building, but it was relatively attractive, and relatively affordable, so we decided to go for it.

And then that other shoe dropped! Our application was declined. We had no other option but to look elsewhere, however, so we trudged ahead. A few days later, we came across a much more attractive office building in the area with a sign that indicated available space from 900 to 10,000 square feet. The smallest space would have been perfect, but with my bruised self-confidence, I was reluctant to apply. Delane's faith prevailed, however, and we did, in fact, apply to lease the space. By the grace of God, we were approved! We moved into our new digs two weeks later… and not too long after that, we redecorated our living and guest rooms. Delane was delighted.

Now, it might seem like a small thing, to be approved by a landlord to lease a "very small" office space, but it was much more than that. You see, we were to get a lead on our largest potential client to date a few weeks later, and the first item on his agenda was to fly over from Los Angeles to meet with us at our office—and now we actually had one (but more on that later). More important than that, however, was God's hand in finding this building and office space for us in the first place, only by having our application denied when we'd applied for our first choice.

This was a Class A building of several hundred thousand square feet in the heart of Scottsdale, Arizona. It had a soaring, three-story interior atrium, accentuated by fifteen-foot palm trees and water features of rippling brooks and cascading waterfalls that tumbled over rocky paths creating a soothing, bubbling sound. When you entered, it seemed like an oasis after the hot, sunny Arizona landscape outside, and its effect was to provide the most professional and upscale impression imaginable!

What we didn't know at the time was that this would be ParaWest's home for the next twenty-plus years. Yes, as we've grown, we've been able to expand into adjacent space, multiplying our office space several times over in one of the most desirable buildings in Scottsdale, Arizona, all because God had known better, and He had a better plan!

GOD NOTE

Angels in Disguise

One of the greatest personal blessings we received when we started ParaWest and moved into our new office was the love and company of our then-two-year-old Shih Tzu (pronounced Sheet Zue), Sadie Bell. Sadie Bell was twelve pounds of snuggle, with mostly black, soft, curly fur, and white spots on her chest and right rear foot. She was adorable.

When we first got Sadie Bell, we had wanted a puppy that could travel with us so we could take her anywhere. Shih Tzus, it turns out, are just the thing for that. They are perfect travelers: quiet and mindful, and they love to lie in their traveling abodes known as "Sherpa bags." These are airline-approved carry-ons into which they can climb and sleep comfortably anywhere, any time. Sadie Bell loved hers, and we took her everywhere.

Well, we almost didn't lease the office at the building we had found because when we went to sign the lease, we were told we couldn't add a clause allowing us to bring Sadie Bell into the office with us. We were told, however, that while it couldn't be added to the lease, we'd probably be okay if we simply were discreet. So we considered the alternative and moved forward with the lease.

For the next fourteen years, we took Sadie Bell with us to the office every day. We'd carry her into the building in her Sherpa bag, and she'd have the office as her home for the day. We were blessed to have her there, as any pet lover knows, as she was always a calming and uplifting influence on a hectic day or among the stresses of running a business. She was also a great hostess, greeting anyone who came to the office with her puppy-dog eyes and a wag, and people loved it as she brightened their own hectic days.

Now, some say puppy dogs might be God's angels in disguise. Well, I don't know about that, but I do know that Sadie Bell brought a little heaven into our world each day, and we thank God for blessing us with her!

CHAPTER 5

On Our Way

According to a study published by the "Big Four" accounting firm, Deloitte, while 86 percent of companies believe that succession planning is "urgent" and an "important priority," only 14 percent believe they do it well. As ParaWest enters its third decade, succession will be essential to our long-term success.

Shortly after ParaWest's twentieth anniversary, Delane and I promoted "Kim" to be a managing partner of ParaWest, along with our other newly appointed co-managing partner (but more on that later). We were thrilled to bestow this honor on Kim as we looked toward the next generation of ParaWest, but twenty years prior, as we started ParaWest with three clients and five employees, we had no inkling this would someday occur. And here's what led up to that.

We did, in fact, end up meeting with that potential new client who wanted to fly over and meet us at our office. It was August 2003, and we had been in our new offices for about two weeks. The space was modest, but professional, and that, combined with the prestige that came from officing in a building of this caliber, was everything we needed.

This potential client had ten apartment properties scattered throughout the Phoenix and Tucson metro areas. They ranged in size from just over one hundred apartments to the largest at just under five hundred units. This was a tremendous opportunity for our fledgling company. The client had been referred to us by an employee of one of his apartment buildings who had worked with Delane in the past and knew her and her capabilities well. So we also had a lot of credibility going into our initial discussions and meeting with him.

To make a long story short, our meeting went well, and he decided to give us a chance. He retained us to manage his largest property (i.e., 483 apartments), with the understanding that if we did a good job on getting occupancy and income up there, he would turn over the management of others to us as well.

Clearly, God's hand was all over this, from generating the referral by a trusted former colleague, to providing us with the professional setting to meet, and then providing us with an opportunity through which we were bound to succeed because of the needs of the property and our experience in operating similar apartment properties in this market. So we assumed the management of this property, and we succeeded rapidly, increasing occupancy from 80 percent when we started to 95 percent in less than ninety days. True to his word, our new client then turned over his other buildings to our management, and we now had more than two thousand apartment units under management. We were on our way!

But this wasn't our greatest blessing in all of this. You see, when he awarded us the contract to manage the 483-unit apartment community, we had no employee with the experience and ability to serve as a manager of this size community, which was considered quite large as apartment communities go. We needed a very competent, experienced manager to be able to succeed, and we had to recruit someone new. Our success or failure would be dependent on this new employee's ability to do the job!

Now, Delane has always been the "people person" between the two of us. She made a career by recruiting, hiring, training, and developing talented candidates. She was the "mentor." So she began her outreach and search, and successful it was, indeed, beyond our wildest expectations! You see, the "manager" she hired in August 2003, Kim, is today our "managing partner of operations" for ParaWest.

Kim excelled in her first position in Phoenix, and in 2008, she moved to open our Houston office. A few years after that, we expanded her responsibilities and promoted her to "associate partner," and in 2023, we then promoted her to her current position as managing partner.

Kim has been integral to every piece of business and growth we've achieved over these many years. So while we thought we were just hiring a manager for a 483-unit apartment community, God's plan was much, much greater, as He brought her to us way back then, then led us to work together in so many successful ways to get to where we are today. It was God's plan all along!

GOD NOTE

And on the Seventh Day, He Rested

During the second year after Delane and I had started ParaWest, we spent a long weekend in Telluride, Colorado. It was one of the few times we had gotten away for pleasure during those early years before we had supervisors to oversee things in our absence, and we were working six and sometimes six and a half days a week while growing and establishing our business.

Telluride, originally a mining town, is a heavenly little Western town with a main street lined with shops and restaurants, and resort accommodations higher up the mountain that you get to by riding the aerial tram. It's located in southeast Colorado in the Rocky Mountains, and we were able to make the eight-hour drive there in only six and a half hours. It was a wonderful place to spend a three-day weekend.

We spent the weekend enjoying God's creation with views of the snow-capped Rockies from our hotel. Across the valley from our hotel suite we could see a magnificent Rocky Mountain landmark that, we were told, was represented in the picture found on the front of Coor's Light beer cans. It was beautiful. We enjoyed the restaurants and the tram, and we hiked to a gorgeous waterfall nearby. After spending weeks and months on our newly started business, it was a delightful and relaxing weekend, and yes, Sadie Bell went with us.

The drive to and from Telluride from our home in Scottsdale took us north through Flagstaff, then through an area that included a large expanse of the Navajo Indian Reservation (i.e., the "Navajo Nation"), then northeast through "Four Corners," where four state boundaries meet—including Arizona, New Mexico, Utah, and Colorado—and finally along the Rocky Mountain foothills to the quaint town of Telluride. The Navajo Reservation is vast, encompassing more than twenty-five thousand square miles, approximately the size of West Virginia, so a large part of the drive to Telluride winds through it.

Within this vast reservation, there are many lakes and streams, as well as several National Monuments, but not along the lonely stretch of highway we were traveling. The route was dotted with traditional "Hogans," circular structures of wood or cement with a smoke hole in the center of the roof, and the landscape along this route consists of arid and rocky land, with little other development to be seen. But the vast, arid land has a certain beauty derived from its rocky crags, hills, and mesas accented by red and golden hues that cast an ethereal glow at dusk, kind of otherworldly.

Well, we were driving home in the early evening that Sunday after a wonderful weekend when He first whispered. We were traversing the reservation on that lonely stretch of highway and enjoying the otherworldly landscape, when the highway took us past a small church—more of a chapel, really.

It was a small wood-sided chapel with a traditional steeple rising from the roof and a simple cross on top. But it wasn't the chapel that caught my eye so much as the large, wooden sign that had been erected in the parched ground in front. Painted in solid black letters on the stark, white, wooden sign were the words, "Keep the Sabbath Holy."

Now, such a simple message might not usually have much of an impact, but on that particular Sunday in that particularly lonely place, it reached out to me as if it were coming from a Jumbotron at a football stadium. God was speaking to me.

You see, Delane and I had been attending our church for years—not every Sunday, but some. But with the startup of ParaWest, we had spent more and more Sundays working on "catchup to dos" and less on rest, worship, and time in His Word. And so it hit me. It was as clear as a bell.

On that Sunday, on that far-away reservation, my heart had been convicted, and I vowed then and there that I would no longer work on Sundays, that I would keep the Sabbath holy, and that I would "rest" as God intended. God had whispered, and I had listened. And for the following twenty-something years, Delane and I have kept that vow, and we are thankful for it.

CHAPTER 6

Spreading Our Wings

It was 2007, and ParaWest had just assumed the management of our first apartment property in Houston, Texas, a city twice the size of Phoenix, with one of the most dynamic economies in the United States and a growing population base, a great place to be in the apartment business. What a blessing this would be! It would be the first of more than a hundred apartment properties we would manage in Texas and the surrounding states over the upcoming years. We hadn't planned on spreading our wings and branching outside of Arizona, and we certainly hadn't foreseen where such an expansion would lead, but here's what led up to that.

We had grown our management portfolio in Arizona over the past few years, and we were doing well there, when, out of the blue, one of our clients came to us and asked if we would consider expanding into Houston, Texas, where he was looking to buy his next apartment property. He explained that his research had indicated that Houston was an "up and coming" apartment market, due to its growing employment base and increasing population, all of which led him to conclude that it would be a good place to invest in apartments.

Delane and I had managed in cities outside of Arizona in the past, including Las Vegas, Albuquerque, Santa Fe, Pasadena, and a few others, so we weren't gun-shy about venturing out of our backyard, but we had not planned to venture so far afield with our new company, ParaWest. No, we had never considered this as a growth direction for our thriving new company, but now a *whisper* was prodding us. So we agreed to work with this client and start operations in Houston.

We considered what it would take to travel to Houston and manage an apartment community long distance, with a two-hour flight each way. We would each have to take on partial responsibility, so that neither would have to bear the burden of the travel excessively. We'd have to hire local talent in Houston to manage the property from day to day, we'd have to learn the market and its nuances for marketing, and we'd have to find local vendors for supplies and services.

Our client had expressed that this property was expected to be only the first of several he wanted to purchase there, so, from a business perspective, the expansion would provide growth opportunities for ParaWest. In addition to all this, we recognized that Houston was a much more opportunistic market than Phoenix or Tucson because of its size and economy; it was one of the top three job-producing metro areas in the United States.

We had heard God's *whispers*, but He had much more in mind, because shortly after acquiring his first property there, the client who had asked us to manage property in Houston came back to us with a new proposal. He wanted us to partner with him in purchasing additional apartment communities in Houston. The proposal was not for us to invest in these acquisitions, but rather, to partner with him as joint managing members for the properties, in order to operate them.

We would raise the capital to purchase the properties through investors he knew, and for putting the deals together with him and operating the apartment communities for the groups of investors, we would gain a minority ownership interest in the deal. What an opportunity this was! We had the experience and the know-how to do the job, but we had not been actively involved in ownership up to that point because the capital requirements for larger apartment communities (in the tens of millions) was beyond our reach.

We hadn't planned on going into apartment ownership when we started ParaWest, although if we could have, we would have. Nevertheless, here was a tremendous opportunity that came to us from out of the blue. We hadn't expected it, we hadn't planned it, but God had! It had been His plan all along.

So, 2007 was a banner year for ParaWest, with opportunities coming from directions we never expected, and doors opening that we never knew were there. As ParaWest grew and prospered, we were seeing God's hand in all of it, and it looked like a grand plan, indeed!

CHAPTER 7

Water: The Substance of Life

Imagine a twelve-year-old child living in a third-world country who has to get up at dawn every day—not to get ready for school, but to take her empty jug and walk ten miles to the nearest water well, pump the water to fill her jug, then walk back home so her family can make it through another day.

Yes, water truly is "the substance of life"! In many third-world countries, however, clean, safe drinking water is hard to come by. In rural Zambian villages in sub-Saharan Africa, many school-age children can't attend school because they have to walk so many miles each day to the nearest water source, usually a water well installed by an NGO (non-government organization, i.e., a charity). These organizations can't afford to install wells in every rural village in Africa, so they're often miles apart.

In the early fall of 2007, however, one small rural village called "Maimbo," not far from Lusaka, the capital of Zambia, in south-central Africa, got their own well and pump, and their children no longer had to make the daily walk to provide for each family's needs. That water well was our first foray into helping to support an international ministry, as Delane and I had made the decision to fund the well through an international charitable organization known as Bread and

Water for Africa. Our prayer was to give this gift of life to these villagers who lived halfway around the world from us as a way to extend God's blessings, which had been so bountiful in our own lives. And here's what led up to that.

By 2007, our business, ParaWest, was growing and thriving. Over the past four years, we had been working with two local Phoenix faith-based ministries, one known as the Bridge, and the other, Mentor Kids USA, for which we provided transportation (i.e., chartered buses) for summer and holiday outings for disadvantaged elementary-age kids. Our eyes were opened widely, however, when Delane came home from a business conference one day in early spring with a new idea, a *whisper*. At the conference, they had been discussing international charities, and she came home with the fresh idea that the money we used for charitable donations could go much further in many impoverished third-world countries. Since we didn't want to curtail our local outreach, we decided to continue with those while expanding with our first international outreach.

As we began our research, we learned that most African countries were at the bottom of the economic ladder and the top of the poverty levels, with many basic human needs, such as clean water, basic hygiene, nutrition, health care, and others, going unmet. It was an easy decision to look toward Africa to broaden our outreach, but where to start? As we continued our research, a *whisper* provided direction.

Several years ago, long before we had started ParaWest, we had managed apartments that were part of an affordable housing division of a large international charity. We had known the CEO of that charity for years and had become friends. We knew the organization worked in Africa, but we had no idea what they actually did. So we decided to reach out and ask.

We called our friend and told him what we were thinking, which was to start by offering a modest grant and to continue with financial aid on an annual basis to a worthy cause. We were quite pleasantly surprised at his receptive response, which was entirely supportive of our efforts and plan, as he told us about their activities in Africa.

We learned they had a separate division known as Bread and Water for Africa (BWA), which partnered with local ministries in thirteen different African countries, and their efforts spanned a broad range, from providing clean water, to agricultural assistance, as well as schools, orphanages, and more. Who knew? We had thought reaching out to them was a long shot, but we'd try anyway. But God knew, and God led us.

Our friend suggested that he put us in touch with the organization's director overseeing BWA. He further suggested that BWA could do an RFP (request for proposal) in reaching out to the local ministries on our behalf, and then we could decide which proposal was the best fit for our goals and make our decision accordingly. So he put us in touch with Beth, who ran BWA, and Beth led us in creating an RFP for her to distribute to their ministries and solicit proposals for our consideration. In early July 2007, we received an email with seven individual proposals from ministries in seven different African countries for our review and consideration. We were overwhelmed!

The range of requests was amazing—from school and medical supplies, to agricultural equipment, building improvements at orphanages, water wells, and more, far too many alternatives to list here. So we read, discussed, and prayed, and as we did so, we narrowed our objectives to include "helping children" in a meaningful and godly way, and we decided to start with "basic needs," because if you don't have clean water or food, not much else matters.

We drew inspiration from a quote by Mother Teresa, paraphrased as follows: *"The poor don't need our pity or our sympathy, they need our love… they need our help!"*

Another objective, perhaps more on the selfish side, was that we wanted to serve in a country at least reasonably safe enough for us to travel to, so we could meet the people we were to serve, learn more about their needs, and share their lives. Africa can be a beautiful continent, but many of its countries are hotbeds of civil war, terrorism, and all kinds of atrocities.

After much consideration, we decided on the well in the village outside Lusaka, Zambia. Zambia is a democratic country, predominantly Christian, and reasonably safe to travel to, although that is difficult, with its location in south-central Africa in the middle of a very large continent. The proposal came from the founder of Kabwata Orphanage and Transite Centre, Angela Miyanda (but more on that later). The orphanage was located in the city of Lusaka, but Angela also served the impoverished rural villages outside of Lusaka as part of her ministry. This was where God had led us.

So in late 2007, our well was installed and operational. We sent a brass plaque all the way from Scottsdale to attach to the pump. The plaque was engraved with the following inscription:

Jesus said to them… whoever believes in me shall never thirst.
— John 6:35 (ESV)

To all who drink from this well, "May Life Abundant begin for you today!"

Dedicated by: ParaWest Community Development, Scottsdale, AZ, USA

Our first foray into international ministry was underway, and it would lead to much more over the next seventeen years. God had whispered, and God had provided! ParaWest was His!

CHAPTER 8

And Then Some

L anding that first big client is a major step for most fledgling companies.

Microsoft landed IBM early on in one of the most Samson-and-Goliath stories in corporate history. In 1980, Microsoft was a five-year-old startup tech company with forty employees and hadn't yet developed its first operating system. At that time, IBM was the largest company in the world, with a market cap of thirty-five billion dollars (128 billion in today's dollars), but despite its size and market depth, it was behind in entering the personal computer market. As it prepared to launch its first PC, IBM needed a software operating system. And that's where Microsoft entered the picture, by purchasing an operating system from another company, renaming it MS-DOS, and licensing it to IBM for its new computers. With that early move, a star was born, and Microsoft grew into arguably one of the most successful companies in corporate history.[3]

On a much smaller scale, a friend of ours with a relatively small landscape architectural design company landed the contract for the landscape design of Apple headquarters, a coup well beyond their expectations at the time.

Keeping a big client is just as important as landing it, and often both landing and keeping that big client can come from the most unexpected places or developments. For the past eighteen years, ParaWest has had one client and partner that has stood above the rest in terms of the amount of business we have done together. We have worked together as both manager and client and as co-owner partners and manager. In addition to those relationships, he has referred other owners to us who have needed management services. Over the years, this has been a very successful relationship for both of us, and we have been very blessed along the way. It had, however, come out of nowhere. We hadn't seen it coming, and it hadn't seemed to start out as a long-term dynamic opportunity. Who would have known? Yes, God had known all along, and here's what led up to that.

Yes, 2007 was a banner year indeed. We were spreading our wings and then some. So when 2008 started out just as strong, our confidence was running high. As the year started, another key opportunity came to us. An apartment mortgage broker whom our partner-client knew and worked with referred us to a potential new client who was purchasing his first property in Houston and needed a management company. Because this was a referral from a credible source whom the buyer already knew, we had a strong chance of landing this contract.

We initiated discussions with the potential new client, and soon learned he was looking at this only as a short-term arrangement. He explained that he was new in apartment investing after having recently sold another successful business. His objective was to hire us to manage the property for a year; during that time he wanted to "shadow" our personnel and learn the business, so he could then manage the property on his own without our services. He further explained that he would then be acquiring additional properties in Houston, but he would no longer need our services for those properties.

Well, since this was our first new opportunity in this new Houston market, and since a year was better than nothing, we agreed and accepted his conditions. As we began working with him, we found him to be very intelligent, but more importantly, we found him to be a very upstanding kind of individual in all our interactions. He was respectful of our personnel, mindful of not interfering with daily operations as he set about to learn the business.

And set about it he did. He set up his desk in the apartment community office across from our manager so he could observe everything. Now, there was nothing wrong with his intentions or his approach, but for a twenty-something-year-old manager to have her boss/client observing her every move, it had to be intimidating. But with no alternative, she went about setting up operations on her new property and working with the residents, vendors, and maintenance and leasing personnel in managing this property. Being a very detailed and methodical manager, she was extremely effective with all this, and soon she had the property fully occupied and looking better than ever. All along, our client observed, interacted when asked, and set about to learn the business so he could do it on his own.

Now, from initial appearances, managing an apartment community of 120 units might seem to be a pretty easy job. You rent the apartments, collect the rent, direct your maintenance team to make repairs as needed and requested, and call vendors when needed, and, well, that's about it. In reality, however, apartment management is an extremely diverse occupation requiring skills across a broad spectrum, including financial management, personnel management, people skills, sales skills, dealing with emergencies, and many, many more. It's a 24/7 occupation, as residents live in their apartments and may need assistance for maintenance, emergencies, or other problems at any time night or day. It is a tough job, and it takes a real professional to do it well. And ours was a pro.

So, long story short, although our client was a hard worker and well-intentioned, long before that first year ended, he had determined that while owning apartments as an investor was what he wanted to do, apartment management surely wasn't for him. And he told us so. He told us he'd be continuing to retain us and utilize our services going forward. And so he did, and that's what we've done for eighteen years now—and we're still going. Who would have known? God knew—yes, it was His plan all along!

GOD NOTE

Wonders

We saw the mist rising into the dusty African air hundreds of feet above the falls as our Zambian Airways Haviland Dash 8 made its final approach for landing in Livingstone. Below us, a short distance away was Victoria Falls, one of the Seven Wonders of the World. We were heading to see the falls and the surrounding area for two days of respite after spending a week at Kabwata Orphanage and the surrounding rural villages, getting to know the kids and learning about the program's needs for our future planning. The trip was an unexpected blessing that had come about from our involvement with Bread and Water for Africa and their African ministries. And what a blessing it was!

We hadn't expected this; however, on our first visit there, we learned the people of Zambia have a strong national pride in their heritage and in their country's beauty, and Victoria Falls was the pinnacle of that pride. So, when we originally scheduled our trip, Angela, who ran the orphanage, planned this short visit for us to experience this wonderous sight. And what a wonder it was! As we approached the falls in our Jeeps from the airport, the roaring thunder grew louder and louder, and the rising mist got denser and more cloud-like. It quickly became evident as to why this colossal flow of water had been proclaimed one of the Seven Natural Wonders of the World.

For the record, the Zambian folks proudly claim that the views are best from their side, but I can't attest one way or the other on that.

The falls were discovered by the British missionary and explorer Dr. David Livingstone in 1855 when they first became known to the

Western world. And what a discovery it was. The falls stretch for more than a mile on the Zambezi River along an escarpment traversing the border between Zambia and Zimbabwe. The cascading water plunges dramatically into the Batoka Gorge from heights reaching up to 354 feet, and the falling water creates a deafening roar and a rising mist that can be seen for miles. The main curtain of the falls is aptly named Devil's Cataract, and the display is known in a local dialect as *Mosi-oa-Tunya*, or "the Smoke That Thunders."

As you approach the falls on the walkway in this national park, plastic ponchos are provided to keep from getting soaked from the mist, which becomes more of a rainstorm the closer you get to the falls. From the vantage point at the top of the falls, you can see the lengthy cascade of water accented by rainbows above, which are created from the sun shining through the mist. It's mesmerizing.

Descending the trail that leads to the bottom of the falls unveils an entirely different experience. As you descend, you enter an ever-thickening rainforest of green plants and trees that appear to reach out and envelop the trail. It's an awe-inspiring experience, and by the time you reach the bottom, the glory of the majestic falls rising above you leaves you utterly breathless. And *breathless* aptly describes the hike back up the steep trail through the steamy rainforest, but it is worth every bit of sweat and heavy breathing that's required.

The hike to and from the falls revealed other African highlights. Monkeys scurried up and down the trees around the trail, and the not-so-occasional baboons along the trail certainly gave us a start as we stepped aside to let them pass. Later that evening in our nearby resort, we would be entertained by zebra moms and babies wandering through the grassy areas between the buildings. In our world, truly an unusual spectacle.

So, there we were, and our two days at Victoria Falls had been beyond our expectations. We would go on to other travel adventures on our future visits to Kabwata Orphanage, including safaris that would leave us in awe of the wonders of Africa and create memories of this glorious continent that we would cherish for the rest of our lives. Yes, Africa was part of our adventure in so many ways—and in so many ways yet to come.

Six-year-old Michael at Kabwata Orphanage,
Lusaka, Zambia

Author Michael and his wife, Delane,
shown in original ParaWest brochure photo, 2003

Sadie Bell, ParaWest's friendly greeter

Michelle, her boys, and their church family
at her graduation from the Bridge
(Michelle is on the right,
with Daniel, Nathan, and Bazil bottom left)

Victoria Falls, one of the Seven Wonders of the World, located on the border between Zambia and Zimbabwe in South-Central Africa

Top of Victoria Falls with rainbows and rising mist

God Whispers Are Life Changers

First water well in Zambia. From left: president of Bread and Water for Africa; Paul, headman of Maimbo Village; author; Angela Miyanda

Headman, Paul, and son

Group of huts in Maimbo Village, also known as nkatas

God Whispers Are Life Changers

PART II
Famine

CHAPTER 9
The World Turns

Yes, 2008 started out as another banner year. Not only did we start with our new client "shadowing" us while we worked, but we were also soon moving forward with our first acquisition in Houston with our other partner. This would be our first ownership opportunity, and we were hopeful of much more of this business to come.

We worked hard through the first half of the year and made our first trip to Zambia to visit Kabwata Orphanage and the villages nearby in early fall. Delane stayed home to run the business, as it was too soon for ParaWest for both of us to be gone at the same time, so we decided on me traveling for this trip (but more on that later). Then, in September 2008, the world turned, badly, and ParaWest's world with it. By the end of 2009, ParaWest had lost nearly 60 percent of its business. We were back to 2005 levels, and here's what led up to that.

It was the start of the "Great Recession," the deepest, most impactful economic downturn since the original Great Depression in 1929. We hadn't seen it coming. No one had. In September 2008, Lehman Brothers, the fourth-largest investment bank in the world, failed and went out of business. The financial effects rippled through the U.S. economy, first through other banks, then through businesses and employment, and eventually around the world, as no country's economy was immune.

The U.S. stock market plunged by 50 percent, and unemployment soared to 10 percent and even higher in many cities. The apartment market was shattered, as renters could no longer afford to pay their rent without jobs, and capital markets no longer had any liquidity for apartment owners to sell their financially distressed properties. Mortgage payments couldn't be made, and property owners went into default, many of them facing foreclosure.

Phoenix was hit particularly hard by the recession. Its economy at that time was driven strongly by growth; hence, new construction and all the jobs it generates was its largest employer. Just under three hundred thousand jobs were lost almost overnight. As development ground to a complete stop, unemployment soared, topping out above 11 percent. The Phoenix apartment market occupancy levels tanked, resulting in severe economic losses for owners. No one was immune.

As the economic performance of properties decline, owners look first to property management as the culprit and the first line of change. *Maybe someone else can do better* is the thinking, and with nowhere else to turn for relief, owners often change their management companies. In ParaWest's case, there was another factor in play. Our largest client, whom we had now worked for successfully for five years, had brought on board an assistant to advise him in overseeing his properties (i.e., overseeing our work). In hindsight, it reminded me of the story in Genesis in the Bible about Joseph, and paraphrasing: "There came into Egypt a Pharaoh he did not know" (see Exodus 1:8). While Joseph's family and relatives lost their freedom and became slaves, ParaWest lost its management contracts.

So our income plummeted. Employees were laid off as we adjusted to this economic environment, and we regrouped to seek out new business opportunities in this depressed economy. We went back to the basics, meeting with real estate professionals to generate referrals and initiating contact with apartment owners whose properties were suffering economically. So, we started to rebuild, but it was not an easy road. The depressed economy plodded along, and we would later see that Phoenix's employment levels would not return to pre-recession levels for more than six years.

Houston, on the other hand, ended up being one of the least-impacted metro areas in the nation, and it saw employment return to pre-recession levels after only one year; then it grew from there. So, this had been God's plan all along, and while we hadn't seen it beforehand, He had, as He had led us into the Houston market the year before. Without this move, it's likely that ParaWest would have perished during the Great Recession, along with hundreds of other businesses that didn't make it through.

GOD NOTE

The Old Man
and the Sea

It was July fifth, just four months after we had started ParaWest, and we were in Florida, having attended a family reunion the day before. It was 6:30 a.m., and we were leaving Daytona Harbor on my first-ever deep-sea fishing charter. There were several family members on board, including Delane, her father, our two sons, and our niece.

As we motored slowly out of the harbor into the Atlantic Ocean, we were awestruck. The ocean was as smooth as glass, something I had thought never occurred in the Atlantic, and although the sun was up, it hadn't yet poked through the dense, vapory fog that hugged the water as we glided through it. By the time we reached our fishing grounds, thirty miles out and an hour later, the fog had cleared, waves were starting to roll, and we were ready to fish.

We had only taken these few days off from our new business because of the family reunion hosted by Delane's parents that Fourth of July, which we would never have considered missing. And with only a few properties in our portfolio, we were able to cover things while we were away. So, there we were on a beautiful, sunny July day on the water.

It didn't take long for us to start getting strikes. Within the first hour, we had landed several mackerel and one very big, very scary-looking barracuda. If you've never seen a barracuda, they're long—this one was about five feet—they have narrow bodies, and the scary part is their huge, four-inch-long, pointy teeth that look like they could slash a human limb at will. Several times that morning, when we had gotten a smaller fish on our hook, a giant barracuda came along and chomped it in half, and we ended up landing half a fish when all was said and done.

The highlight of the day, however, was the big Dorado I had the pleasure and adventure of catching. A Dorado, also known as a mahi-mahi, is a spectacularly colored fish, with a bright yellow underbelly, a phosphorescent blue streak above, and a large green dorsal fin on top. It's a beautiful fish, whose name comes from the Hawaiian language and means "very strong." And strong he was!

Because we were using relatively light tackle and line-targeting reef fish, this 55-pound trophy would "run" every few minutes, pulling out reels and reels of line on our light drag. Every time I'd get him close to the boat, he'd run. This went on for more than a half hour before we finally got him landed, and all that time, I'd be reeling, reeling, reeling, and sweating, sweating, sweating, until by the end of it, I was totally exhausted and utterly spent. But it had been worth it, and Delane's immediate reaction was, "Let's have it mounted and take it home!"

So, fast-forward to 2020, during the height of the pandemic, when we were blessed to be able to renew our Scottsdale office lease for ParaWest, and as part of our renewal, we received a handsome "tenant improvement allowance" to remodel and redecorate our offices. And so we did, and in the process, we built a large new conference room complete with a glass wall entrance and new furniture. And you guessed it, we hung that beautiful, 55-pound yellow, blue, and green Dorado on our new conference room wall. Oh, and a few years after catching the Dorado, we added a mounted Pacific blue marlin that we caught off Cabo San Lucas, Mexico, making it a set.

Now, I don't know whether God had a hand in our catching that fish on that July day long ago, or if He just let our free will get lucky, but I'd like to think He was certainly there smiling, knowing that we'd be blessed with that beautiful masterpiece of creation adorning our conference room wall all those years later. On second thought, I'm sure He was!

CHAPTER 10

Two Are Better Than One

Two are better than one, because they have a good reward for their toil. For if they fall, one will lift up his fellow. But woe to him who is alone when he falls and has not another to lift him up!

—Ecclesiastes 4:9–10 ESV

As I explained earlier, shortly after the twentieth anniversary of ParaWest, Delane and I promoted Kim to managing partner. At the same time, we appointed Christopher (Chris) as a managing partner, as well. Together these two managing partners make an incredible team, with experience and knowledge in the apartment business that places them among the top tier in this industry, and few could surpass them. They also have very complementary skills and abilities, similar to the complementary skills Delane and I had brought to our new company twenty years prior.

Having mentored under Delane for many years, Kim had top-notch people and organizational skills, while Chris is outstanding on the financial, investment, and construction side. And as King Solomon expressed in Ecclesiastes nearly three thousand years ago: "Two are better than one." So, as with Delane and me before them, Kim and Chris would lead ParaWest into the future with their complementary skills and leadership acumen.

It was an easy decision for Delane and me, and we knew it had come from Him. As I described Kim's starting with ParaWest in our first year, when we had no idea of where things would lead, and no intention of one day appointing her as managing partner, Chris's start would be even more tenuous and seemingly even less likely to result in his earning his eventual managing partner position. But earn it he did, and here's what led up to that.

Chris graduated from college in 2007 with a business degree and a double major in real estate and social science. Chris is our youngest son—my stepson. During his last semester, he interned with a non-profit company that developed apartment communities for seniors, among other things. Chris was interested in development, and after finishing his degree, he started his job search. Now, Delane and I had never wanted to steer our sons into our business, as we wanted them to pursue their own interests and passions, so we had never actually discussed Chris coming to work with us at ParaWest.

Well, as most career people in any occupation come to learn, finishing your degree is only a start. That enables you to obtain an entry-level position in whatever field you're entering, and you must make your way up the ladder from there. So, Chris was beating the bushes looking for an entry-level job, but the pickings were slim. He had an offer as an entry-level analyst at a real estate statistics firm, a company that published stats on all different metrics of the real estate market... not really what he wanted. So, while he was searching and waiting for the right opportunity, we approached him about taking on a temporary position with ParaWest to fill his time and provide him with some spending money.

The position was at the property Kim managed, with 483 apartments in west Phoenix. Since we had assumed the management of the property four years prior, one building, out of the thirty-six buildings on the site, had sat empty. It had thirty-two apartments and had been severely damaged by a fire long before we got involved; it had remained in that condition for years. Because the rest of the property was doing well financially under our management by then, the owner asked us to take on renovating the building and putting the apartments back into a new condition so they could be rented out.

So, we offered this development position to Chris, to contract out the demolition of the fire-damaged interiors and then rebuild those apartments to rent them out. It was a challenging undertaking, requiring him to inspect the apartments and write up a "scope of work" in order to bid the work to subcontractors, create a budget, and then contract with them to do the work. Additionally, all this would be done under the watchful oversight of the Phoenix Building Department, with their inspectors having to approve every step.

Chris accepted the position and took on the challenge with gusto. In a little less than 120 days, he had those apartments back online and ready to rent. He was quite pleased with his work, as were we, as was our owner/client. Little did we know that over the next fifteen years, Chris would oversee more than seventy million dollars in renovation projects on apartment communities we managed. No, when he finished the job, Delane and I assumed he'd move on to his entry-level position and start his chosen career. But God had other plans.

Shortly after Chris finished rebuilding the thirty-two units, Kim came to us on his behalf. Now, I don't really know how the conversation between the two of them had come about, but Kim explained to us that he'd like to continue with ParaWest. And there was His *whisper*. We were taken by surprise, and I'm sorry to say that we didn't know what was on our son's mind and heart at the time. Nonetheless, we were delighted at the news, so we proceeded to meet with Chris and discuss a potential position.

The position would be designed exclusively for him, to give him a well-rounded base in the many, many facets of our business. He would start working on-site with Kim, as this nearly-five-hundred-unit property had a large staff of more than twenty workers, and plenty

Michael Salkeld   93 of opportunities to gain experience, from leasing to rent collections, bookkeeping, and resident relations on the management side, and all the various trades on the maintenance side, from painting to carpentry, electrical, plumbing, air-conditioning repair, swimming-pool maintenance, and much, much more. Chris accepted and again started with gusto. Working hand in hand with the various office and maintenance personnel, he would gain an appreciation and level of respect for every job and every worker, an appreciation that would provide important "grounding" as he rose through the ranks of the company.

And that was only the beginning. Over the next fifteen years, Chris would gain experience and proficiency in every facet of our business. He moved from on-site management and maintenance to overseeing renovations, and later he got involved on the investment side of the business, providing analysis for acquisitions and finance, eventually putting deals together as the lead manager, working with investors, lenders, and clients. He took on every challenge with a "can do" attitude and spent many hours off the clock studying areas that were new to him and gaining knowledge and experience that took him light-years beyond the college graduate level.

Chris looked to me as a mentor, and by the time he was promoted to managing partner, he had packed my forty-plus years of experience into fifteen. Through those fifteen years, Chris and Kim had become a solidified team, partners who worked together as effectively as Delane and I had, proving once again that Solomon was correct: "two are better than one."

CHAPTER 11

Gifts of the Spirit

The families had left their home in Myanmar (formerly the British colony known as Burma) a midsized country, slightly smaller than Texas, in southeast Asia located on the north end of the Indian Ocean on the Bay of Bengal, with China bordering it to the northeast. After spending more than a year in a squalid camp in neighboring Thailand, the families had traveled more than eight thousand miles to relocate to their new home in Phoenix, Arizona. They were refugees and had fled their homeland to escape the persecution and social upheaval in their country, as more than one hundred and fifty thousand of their country's men, women, and children had done over the previous three years.

This group included eleven families, made up of forty-four kids and twenty-five adults who had received permission to immigrate to the United States. They had made their way to Phoenix, where they lived together as neighbors in an apartment community. Their names sounded different than many of our American names, names like *Tha Dee Say Toe*, *Nye Meh*, *Tau May Oo*, and others.

On that sun-soaked, 75-degree November Saturday, in the midst of the worst recession in decades, they came together with more than fifty church volunteers for an early Thanksgiving celebration in our backyard. It was a joyous day filled with games, food, music, piñatas, face painting, and wonderful fellowship. We were blessed to be able to host and to participate, and here's what led up to that.

Delane and I had been involved in volunteering and ministry service since we'd first met many years prior. But in September 2009, we decided to take advantage of a personal growth opportunity and attend a meeting at our church in which outreach opportunities would be discussed and presented.

What really drew us to the meeting, though, was the spiritual gifts–assessment program they were presenting. The program was essentially a workbook that provided a kind of personal assessment, similar to what's done with personality or career assessments. Only this program was to help you determine what spiritual gifts you might have and how they suit your personality and experiences—and then, of course, how you might apply them in service.

So, we went and worked through the gifts assessment. Now, there are many spiritual gifts as identified in the Bible, including faith, knowledge, interpretation of tongues, leadership, prophecy, healing, and others. Well, although we've done a lot of volunteer work, I've always struggled to find my most appropriate place. You see, I don't have medical training or carpentry skills or other trade skills. I'm not great at interacting with children. I'm not a natural evangelist. So, in short, I don't seem to have much to offer.

But there was one… no, there were two… that applied to me, where I found my calling, and I've been active in applying these ever since. The first was hospitality, and the second was leadership. Regarding leadership, I've been in leadership positions most of my adult life, and since those early days of ParaWest, even more… in ministries, in my family, and of course, in our work. Regarding hospitality, this was a new revelation to us. We had always loved offering hospitality to others through so many different means, from opening our home for food, fun, and fellowship, to hosting and serving disadvantaged families and children, and others in need. Yes, this was our true calling. God had whispered that evening.

Shortly thereafter, we had our first opportunity to apply this calling, as our church's local outreach leader, who had been part of our church family at the Bridge, approached us about hosting a Thanksgiving event for refugee families whom the church supported. We learned a lot about refugees in planning for that event. We learned that refugees have been around always, from biblical times to the current world. Refugees are often courageous people who leave the home of their families, friends, and ancestors to travel to a new land and home and make a new life. They travel to a new land where they know no one, where they don't speak the language, where they have to learn to live and work. And all because circumstances or events in their homeland made it impossible for them to stay without being severely persecuted, harmed, or even killed. So, they set out in faith and in hope for a better life.

Truly, this refugee ministry to which we had been introduced was a worthwhile and blessed cause. So we looked toward the opportunity with purpose, love, and a joyful spirit, and we weren't disappointed. Eleven refugee families (almost seventy people) arrived at our home that Saturday on the double-decker bus we had chartered for the occasion, appropriately named Divinity Transportation; we had wanted the ride to be as special as the event, and it was. Arriving in comfort and style, the families proceeded to the backyard, where they were welcomed by volunteers.

As this was a Thanksgiving celebration, the yard was adorned with fall decorations; pumpkins were everywhere, along with straw bales, scarecrows, Thanksgiving banners, and of course, six colorful piñatas hanging from a rope on the biggest pine tree many of the kids had ever seen. Volunteers had brought potluck dishes, along with chafing dishes, platters, and bowls of favorite Burmese dishes. Traditional American fare was also lined up on tables along the back of the house. From there we prayed, ate, drank, socialized, played games, and enjoyed the grand finale, which consisted of kids swinging wildly at piñatas dangling from a fifteen-foot branch as they shattered the six piñatas, throwing candy everywhere for them to scatter and collect.

For anyone unfamiliar with piñatas, here's a brief review. Piñatas were brought to Mexico by the Spaniards in the sixteenth century. At the time, they were made of clay vessels filled with various "treasures," used by Spanish monks for evangelism purposes, primarily at Christmas and Eastertime. Piñatas came to the United States later through Mexican immigrants, and they became a party tradition no longer associated with religious holidays. Today's piñata is a papier-mâché figure resembling almost anything—from a donkey, to a star, to a hat. They're about four feet tall, hollow for filling, with the outside colorfully decorated with brightly colored crepe-paper ribbons covering the entire creation. You then fill them with prizes—in this case, hundreds of pieces of wrapped candy.

To play the game, the piñata is tied to a rope that suspends it from a branch or a beam. The kids then take turns being blindfolded, spun in a circle, and then taking three swings of a bat to try to hit it, with the end goal being to break it open so the candies fall to the ground. When they break it, it's a free-for-all, where the kids rush to pick up the pieces until they've got it all. There's also a "trick" involved, because the rope over the branch is held by an adult who can raise and lower the piñata by pulling on it so the blindfolded attacker misses, time and time again, until one gets a lucky hit and shatters the piñata. Without a doubt, the six piñatas that day were the hit of the party. The kids were ecstatic, and the adults were beside themselves, cheering and laughing at every swing, miss, and hit, and especially as the kids mobbed the grassy area for the candy after the piñata gave up its all.

The day was full of many firsts for these new Americans from Burma (Myanmar), from Thanksgiving dishes to new games and most of all, to American Christian hospitality. Yes, it was truly a blessed day during a difficult time in our entrepreneurial adventure, a day that had come about from a *whisper*, and that ended with peaceful and joyous hearts.

God Whispers Are Life Changers

CHAPTER 12

Satan Knocking

It was a trying time for ParaWest going into 2009. As the Great Recession developed, we lost a lion's share of our business, and we had not yet had time to recover and replace it with new business. It was February 2009 when we took on a new client who had been referred to us in Phoenix by an apartment broker we knew. Things moved fast as he retained our services and we took over, initially one property in Phoenix, and shortly thereafter, three more in Tucson.

By March 23, however, just one month later, we had resigned the accounts and parted company. It had been a roller-coaster ride, and not one we'd ever like to repeat. Now, as anyone who strives to live a godly life knows, Satan is always out there, lurking, knocking, and waiting for an opportunity to enter. And there he was, and there he tried. And here's what led up to that.

In early 2009, when a referral from a broker we had known for years came our way, we were elated. The owner had four apartment properties, one in Phoenix and three in Tucson. He initially approached us about managing the Phoenix property, which he had acquired only a few months prior. He had a small, local management company on the property, and things weren't going well. Occupancy was at 78 percent, extremely low even in recessionary times. The property was undergoing a renovation, which was being quite mismanaged, leaving the property in total disarray, with buildings in various stages of renovation. Grounds were strewn with debris, and overall, the operation was disorganized and faltering. It seemed like a good opportunity for ParaWest to take over and implement professional management systems and an organized renovation plan. So we accepted the management assignment, and he retained us for the property.

The warning signs came early on as I spent time with him in discussions about the management of his property. He was a boisterous kind of guy, invoking names of Hollywood celebrities and others whom he had known and hobnobbed with through the years. Now, it's pretty common knowledge in business circles that socializing with clients or potential clients by having a few drinks or dinner is always a good way to start to build rapport and an ongoing relationship, and so we had drinks at a local Phoenix hotel, then I took him to dinner. Delane hadn't joined us, as he seemed more of a "man's man," so to speak.

While we were getting to know one another at dinner, I first heard God's *whisper* telling me to pass on this one and go home. My potential new client was elaborating about his various travels, which he explained had included many trips to Mexico and other destinations with his celebrity friends. On these trips, he bragged, they had great times "whoring around" and indulging in other illicit and unbecoming activities. He elaborated much, much more, things I can't repeat here. Now, I remember very clearly how the hairs on the back of my neck stood up, and I knew when I heard it, that this was very wrong. I'm sure that most folks striving to live a godly life have had the same feeling. It's like "Wow, this really sounds bad," and "Wow, this kind of makes my skin crawl." Satan was knocking, and God was whispering, but I wasn't listening.

So, unfortunately, we assumed the management of his property and went about implementing our management plan. Shortly thereafter, our new client came to us asking us to assume the management of his Tucson properties as well. His partner was managing them at the time, and our client explained that he believed we could do a better job. So, needing the additional business, we moved forward accordingly. His partner, however, did not agree with him on this and was not on board. In order to make this happen, in addition to signing a management agreement with us, our new client took over their joint bank accounts and assumed total oversight. Now, his taking control of their joint bank accounts should have been my second warning that this was not a very forthright guy with whom we were working. But again, I ignored His *whisper*.

We moved forward and assumed management accordingly. Shortly after taking over operations of his Tucson properties, however, our client's partner rebelled and initiated legal action, not against us but against our client. So, within two weeks, we were served a court order requiring us to relinquish management of the Tucson properties and turn it back over to our client's partner.

Not long after that, our concerns about our client's business ethics and directions escalated, particularly related to cash management for the Phoenix property. As managing agents, we handle owners' property funds in our trust accounts at the bank, and we have a fiduciary responsibility to manage the money responsibly. So, anything an owner might do in utilizing property funds for unrelated or untoward purposes could also have an impact on our reputation—or worse. And we would never let that happen. So, before the month was up, we had our attorney draft a letter of resignation, and we resigned the remaining account (i.e., the Phoenix property) on the spot.

Over the following months and years, we would learn through the media that our former client had gotten into all kinds of messes related to these properties. He had filed for bankruptcy, defaulted, and was foreclosed upon on some of the properties; he ended up in lawsuits with Fannie Mae, and he had at least one judgment against him for $2.3 million related to his operation of the properties. There was more, such as allegations of "missing financial records," etc. So God had, indeed, saved us from Satan's knocking on this one. His *whisper* eventually prevailed, and I, in turn, learned to listen more closely and follow His *whispers* in the future.

CHAPTER 13

AWANA

"Approved Workmen Are Not Ashamed"
Paraphrasing of 2 Timothy 2:15 KJV,
by AWANA Clubs International

It was AWANA Pinewood Derby Day at church, and twelve-year-old Scotty had his car ready to race. He was in the sixth grade, his last year of attending AWANA at our church. The Pinewood Derby was a big event for these elementary-aged kids, and there were hundreds of them participating with cars of every shape, color, and design, from a *Toy Story* car, which obviously had been shaped (sawn and carved) by the dad, to Scotty's "military truck" in camo green, which he had fashioned and painted without much of my help.

They raced in groups of ten on the 45-foot downhill track, and with each heat being an eliminating trial, the winners would advance to the next heat and race against other winners, until all but one had been eliminated. There would be trophies for first, second, and third place. Scotty made it through two eliminating heats before being beaten. But he wasn't disappointed at losing—no, he was proud of having won the two heats before that. Yes, it was an incredible day for a twelve-year-old!

If you are unfamiliar, pinewood derby cars are fashioned out of a kit that contains a specific-sized rectangular block of wood, four wheels, axles, and weights to attach to the bottom to create greater speed. The block of wood is 7 inches long and 2¾ inches wide before it's sawn and sanded into finished shape. The maximum weight specified in the rules is "not to exceed five ounces." The kit is then fashioned into a car by the racer, painted appropriately, and entered in the derby. Yes, it was a great day for Scotty and many others at the AWANA Pinewood Derby that year, but that's not what this story's about, because here's what led up to that.

Four years earlier, shortly after we had gotten ParaWest off the ground, our eight-year-old grandson, Scotty, was in the second grade. We wanted to get him more involved in church at that age to help him grow and give him greater purpose and direction. Our church had an AWANA program for pre-K and elementary-aged kids on Wednesday evenings from 6 to 8 p.m.

We were later to learn that AWANA is a sixty-year-old program developed for kids by a group in Chicago initially, and it later spread throughout the United States and eventually the world. The program was designed as kind of a "canned" children's program that individual churches could adapt and modify to their own liking, without having to invent their own programs from the ground up. It was God-inspired, and it included the study and memorization of Bible verses, combined with "message time," then followed by "playtime" consisting of a number of different games held in the gym ranging from dodge ball to tug-of-war, relay races, and many, many more. The program was designed so that by the end of the evening, the kids would go home inspired by the Bible and exhausted from the games. It was great!

Well, as luck would have it, by the time Delane and I thought about getting Scotty involved, it was mid-September, and with the school year having already started, AWANA attendance was maximized, due to the limited number of volunteers and staff running it. However, there was an exception to be made, we learned. If a parent (or, in our case, a grandparent) volunteered to work at the program, their child could still sign up.

Now, I mentioned earlier that I'm not particularly adept at working with kids, and this really wasn't up my alley. But then came the *whisper*.

And after all, who was I to deny our grandson the opportunity to grow with God by spending time each week in AWANA? So, reluctantly, I agreed, and I took on my first second-grade class that fall. It turned out to be a great experience for me, and I participated for the next four years; Scotty did, as well, immersing himself in the program all the way.

So, every Wednesday during the school year for the next four years, Delane and I would pick up Scotty at our son's house, proceed to McDonald's, where he'd have chicken nuggets and we'd dine on burgers and Big Macs, before we headed to AWANA for the evening. It was an exhausting evening, and after the thirty-minute drive to drop Scotty back off at home and then the thirty-minute drive back home, we'd head to bed and pass out immediately.

Now, we had never planned on getting involved in AWANA, and we certainly hadn't known where it would lead, but He had. He had known all along, because we realized along the way, and even more so much later, what godly opportunities He had in store for us.

You see, in addition to our grandson developing a closer relationship with God over those four years, two other incredibly important occurrences would come out of our time in AWANA. The first took place two years after Scotty and I started AWANA, when his younger brother, four-year-old Austin, would also start attending with us on Wednesday evenings, and a year after that, our five-year-old, later-to-be-adopted daughter, Roslyn, would start attending as well (but more on that later). Delane would then become a volunteer leader with AWANA, too, leading Roslyn's class. So, all in all, Wednesday evenings were special for us all for the next few years, as the five of us would head to McDonald's for a scrumptious meal followed by an evening of learning and games at AWANA.

The second important occurrence to come out of this time didn't come to light until five years later. While volunteering at AWANA on Wednesday evenings, we had met and gotten close to our church's children's pastor, Pastor Ryan. Pastor Ryan was great with the kids and the volunteer leaders, and he showed up every Wednesday evening with a smile, a lot of energy, and a passion for working with the kids.

Well, as He would have it, and as He always was ahead of us, we ended up starting a new ministry five years later, a summer program for kids, and we needed classrooms. So we turned to Pastor Ryan for help, and help he gave us. We got the classrooms we needed for our summer program (and more on that later), and AWANA became a part of our story and a part of our adventure as God had led us into uncharted waters working with kids, and He brought us through with all His blessings. Yes, it was another path that we had not intended to go down, and it provided results exceeding anything we could have foreseen.

CHAPTER 14

And It Keeps on Turning

Indeed, the world keeps on turning. By the end of 2009, as the Great Recession surged and we had lost nearly 60 percent of our business, our development efforts had landed us several new clients and properties to manage—in Phoenix, Tucson, and Houston. After it had all shaken out over the following couple of years, by 2011, we had returned to our pre-recession levels and gained some great long-term clients, including one in particular, which truly seemed to be "heaven-sent." And here's what led up to that.

Our marketing outreach in late 2008 and 2009 led us to initiate contact with many different property owners. We knowingly took on some short-term assignments… properties that needed to improve occupancy and income so they could be sold, and as it was relatively early on in our ParaWest adventure, we courted some clients we probably shouldn't have. So, as we took on new properties to manage, some seemed heaven-sent and some… not so much.

The long and the short of it was, we were able to keep ParaWest's doors open during that time, and position our company to be able to take advantage of greater opportunities down the road as the economy improved. And, as an added benefit, we brought on some really great clients during that time of rebuilding. One of those new clients ended up being one of our longest-lasting relationships, and during those somewhat-dark days, they clearly came from God's *whisper*. At the time, they had seemly come from left field, but as events unfolded, this opportunity became clearly from Him.

We had initially approached this owner through correspondence inquiring about his interest in the potential of a client of ours purchasing one of his properties. The owner had five apartment communities—three in Phoenix and two in Tucson. As part of our new-business development process, we had subscribed to a database that provided statistics on apartment properties' occupancy levels, rent rates, and other information, and we were able to use this data to identify financially underperforming properties. These were our "targets," and his were on the list. In addition to the correspondence about a potential purchase, we corresponded about management, offering our services, as we knew his properties were not doing well financially.

Our correspondence continued for several months, but it was one-way only, as he did not respond to our offers or take our calls as we tried to reach out to him. But then, one day in late summer, we received a call. It was from the owner's brother (and partner), who explained that he had been given our name and information by his brother and asked to contact us. He was planning a trip to Phoenix in a few weeks and wanted to meet us and discuss their properties. So we set it up.

Two weeks later, this man and his wife traveled to Phoenix and met with Delane and me and other members of our team. They explained their dissatisfaction with their current management company, and they provided information on their properties, their investment and performance history, and their desire to improve on this, as they were losing money and had a lot invested in these five apartment properties. So, we took them on a tour of a few of our managed properties to show the condition and management of our well-run properties, and then we briefly toured their three Phoenix properties. The meetings and tours were going well.

That's when God showed His hand. They were clearly considering retaining our services, but they hadn't yet fully made up their minds. We had finished touring and were on our way back to our office to continue our discussions—when it happened. I was in the front seat with the owner, and Delane was in the back with the potential client's wife. We were carrying on different conversations, and as we had been together a few hours, topics had drifted from business to other matters of interest. As we were approaching the vicinity of our office, the owner started explaining that they had a friend who lived not far from our office in Scottsdale, with whom they were having dinner that night. This friend was the former pastor of their church in Chagrin Falls, Ohio, where they lived, who had recently taken a position at his new church in Scottsdale.

"Well, that's a coincidence," I said, "because the new pastor of our church in Scottsdale moved here from Chagrin Falls, Ohio." God's *whisper* was suddenly loud, indeed! Our potential new client promptly interrupted the ladies' conversation and promptly explained to everyone in the vehicle that he had just learned that we attended the church *led by their friend and pastor*! At this, his wife, a strong evangelist, took over. As we pulled into our office parking lot, she asked us to pray together. And we did. Then we proceeded to our conference room to discuss their retaining us to manage their properties and to go over an initial timetable and plan. It was an upbeat and inspiring day, and no one in the car that day could have doubted that this meeting was planned by Him. Yes, it had been His plan all along.

Today those clients remain our clients, but more than that, they have become good friends. We've shared good times, and we've worked together in ministries serving others. And all because God brought them to us in our time of need, during one of the darkest economic recessions of the past seventy years.

CHAPTER 15

Sub-Saharan Africa

It was a warm Friday evening in early September 2008, our last night at Kabwata Orphanage and Transit Centre in Lusaka, Zambia, and we were celebrating. We had been in Zambia for a little over a week, spending time with the kids at Kabwata, visiting the village site of our first water well, and gaining an overall understanding of the needs of all there so we could plan further assistance that would prove fruitful. But on that night, we were celebrating!

There were more than sixty kids at the orphanage, ranging in age from toddlers to teens, and six of us from Bread and Water for Africa traveling together. We had purchased pizzas for the kids (a rare treat they never got), and we had dinner on the lawn within the walled-in grounds of the orphanage. After dinner came the entertainment. I was up first, playing my Larrivee guitar with which I often traveled just for fun. "Welcome to My Morning" by John Denver was my opening, followed by some kids' songs, and then the highlight of the evening: "If you're happy and you know it, CLAP YOUR HANDS, STOMP YOUR FEET, SAY AMEN, etc." Much to my surprise, the kids knew it well and stepped up with the loudest, most enthusiastic version I had ever heard. It was exhilarating!

Everyone loved my guitar. In fact, ten years later, when we made our next visit, I played another guitar as we sang together once more. But on that second visit, it was a brand-new Yamaha acoustic model, with a three-piece mahogany back and a resonating spruce front, and we had bought it and brought it to give to the kids. They loved it and sent us a video via email six months later, playing and singing a song they had written.

My music was then followed by the kids, who, we learned, were incredibly musically inclined. They proceeded to put on a show for us. They sang, they danced, and with no other instruments available, some of the boys played drums using upside-down plastic buckets, kind of like those you see when you enter a Home Depot store. They played some of their favorite Zambian traditional songs, some top teen hits, and then a few hymns for us older, more conservative types. They were absolutely awesome! It was a wonderful end to a wonderful week, and here's what led up to that.

We landed in Lusaka after a twenty-two-hour flight on South African Airlines that started in Washington, D.C. We had changed planes in Johannesburg, South Africa. We were met at the airport by Angela, the founder and "mom" of Kabwata Orphanage and Transit Centre, and were taken to our accommodations not far from the orphanage.

These accommodations consisted of a worn-out former British estate that had long since been abandoned by an upper-class British family when Zambia (formerly "Northern Rhodesia") gained its independence in 1964. The grounds were gated and surrounded by a six-foot block wall with razor wire on top to deter the bad guys, which are everywhere in Lusaka, and throughout most of Africa. The swimming pool, which had probably once provided a refreshing respite, was now empty and had grass growing through the concrete, and the grounds were unkempt. The inside was tired but comfortable, and overall, the worn-out, old estate made for great accommodations for the six of us traveling together on our fact-finding mission trip.

The following morning, we began our tour. We started with the orphanage during the first few days, then we took a trip to the rural villages outside Lusaka, including the village of Maimbo, where we'd had the water well installed. We also toured a potential agricultural site, some foster homes where other orphans were living, and a hospice run by Catholic Charities. It was a whirlwind and informative trip, and we learned a lot.

We started with a tour of Kabwata, where we met the "aunties" who took care of the kids and toured the orphanage, and we initially met some of the younger kids as most were in school on a weekday. The orphanage consisted of a walled compound (also topped with razor wire) with several buildings on two acres of grounds. The buildings included two large, dorm-like rooms—one for the boys and one for the girls—and each had more than a dozen bunk beds, with each child having their own private bed. The dorm rooms were neat and clean with beds made, toys in their places, and books on shelves—overall, a great environment for the kids. There was a community kitchen and a large dining room with tables, benches, and inspirational Bible verses decorating the walls. Outside, there were play areas, and a vegetable garden in the back. It was a well-planned and well-kept community home that had evolved through piece-by-piece improvements over many years.

During our week's visit, we came to understand that the kids in Kabwata Orphanage had a better living environment than most children in Lusaka. They were happy kids and had a loving and secure home. They were well-nourished, they had better health care than most of the population, and they attended school nearby, where they were given an education that many kids in Lusaka and the surrounding villages went without. This was truly a blessed home for these children.

We learned that Zambia, like most other countries in Africa, is a nation of orphans, the result of the AIDS epidemic having decimated an entire generation of adults, starting in the 1980s, accelerating in the 1990s, and killing even more in the early 2000s, before finally being relatively abated twenty years later. A census estimate in 2012, a few years after our visit, estimated that 11 percent of Zambia's adult population had been lost to the disease.

We also learned that Zambia is a country of contrasts. In addition to the orphan population creating such a hardship, Zambia's economy and employment potential for adults was among the worst in the world, resulting in more than 60 percent of the population living below the poverty level. On the other hand, Lusaka had some middle-class neighborhoods, with shopping areas much like you'd find in any American suburb.

This contrast became evident when we traveled a mile or two from the middle-class area and found some of the most impoverished neighborhoods on the planet, including ones with no paved roads and are made up of shacks and huts built from discarded wood and aluminum pieces. There are no utilities there; they have centrally located community toilets that service hundreds of families living there. The neighborhoods have no trash service, so residents dump refuse along perimeter streets in piles, which burn day and night and create a horrible stench, sort of like burning rope, that permeates the air all around.

Yes, we learned a lot, and God's *whisper* was on our hearts, assuring us that while we knew we couldn't entirely change this world, we could make life a little better for a handful of innocent children.

We also learned about rural life in Zambia when we visited the villages outside Lusaka. They weren't far—just twenty or thirty miles—but due to the unpaved and poorly graded roads, they took hours to reach in our four-wheel-drive Toyotas. The villagers lived in huts made of mud and grass known as *nkatas*. The huts were round by design, with thatched roofs of straw, and they had dirt floors, with no coverings on the doors or windows. They were built in groups of anywhere from a few to a dozen. They had no water source and, of course, no utilities.

However, one village named Maimbo had a recently installed water well. The well served not only the village of Maimbo, but also several nearby villages that had no water source of their own. The well was proudly presented by the headman of the village, Paul, who showed us the well, the inscribed plaque we had sent, and a nearby garden in which the villagers had recently started to grow vegetables for his family and others. He was a proud man, and he expressed his gratitude for our having provided water for his village. It was a rewarding and eye-opening experience, and we knew we had made the right decision to help these people.

And so now the week was ending, and we were celebrating. We had learned much and made many new friends. We had come to understand that our initial efforts in funding the water well would only be a beginning, and we made the decision to do more in the future, helping both the orphanage and the villages. We hadn't determined exactly what that would entail, but we had a lot to digest and consider.

We also learned that God's *whisper* to us had, indeed, been fortuitous on that day when Delane had come home from a conference in Scottsdale, Arizona, with a new idea about how our dollars would go further in a far-away third-world country. Yes, we had learned a lot. And this was only the beginning!

GOD NOTE
Decimation

It was our first morning in Lusaka, having arrived the evening before, and we were on the patio having breakfast before being picked up for our first tour of Kabwata Orphanage later that day. As I was enjoying my toast, I heard it for the first time—a low, wailing kind of singing coming from the roadway in front of our walled compound. While it sounded kind of eerie, I had no idea what it was. As we left the compound later that morning on our tour, we saw pickup trucks going by with several people in the back of each, singing those low, wailing songs.

When we asked our host about them, we learned they were funeral processions for victims of AIDS. As we drove toward town, she pointed out the cemetery about a mile down the road as we passed, and we could see from our vehicle, mourners huddled together in groups at several different gravesites. We learned that the epidemic was so horrific and widespread that there would be many such funerals each day as friends and family said their last goodbyes to their loved ones who had succumbed to the horrible disease. It was incredibly tragic and saddening.

The first AIDS victim in Zambia had been identified in 1984. The disease spread rapidly after that, and with minimal health care and medicines available to most of its population, fatalities soared. By 2008, the year of our visit, it was estimated that nearly 1.8 million Zambian residents, out of a total population of just over twelve million, had died from the disease. The decimation was staggering, indeed.

Just as sad was the fact that by the early 2000s, AIDS treatments, through improved antiretroviral drugs, were available in most advanced nations. The drug prevented the disease from spreading in the body, giving the infected patient's body the ability to heal its damaged organs, and in most cases, allowing the patient to go on living a normal life. But not in Africa. Not only could African countries and residents not afford the drugs, but malnutrition, which prevented the drugs from having the effect they were designed to achieve, was so prevalent in most African countries that most patients who received the antiretroviral drugs during those years died anyway.

Finally, however, with significant financial aid from the United States and other countries, patients in African nations gained access to both the antiretroviral drugs and to adequate nutritional supplements in their diet to enable the drugs to work, and deaths from the disease started to decline. It's estimated that annual deaths from AIDS in Zambia declined by nearly 80 percent between 2008 and 2023.

Living in the United States, we, of course, were familiar with AIDS and somewhat familiar with its impacts. We had lost loved ones from the disease, as well. But we had no understanding of its much broader impact on Africa, including countries like Zambia, until that visit. And although I would be haunted in the future with dreams of those processions we saw and heard every day while we were there, I take comfort in the brighter side of all this, His *whisper*, assuring our hearts that these children, whom we had been called to help, would have a better life and a brighter future because of our efforts.

CHAPTER 16

California: The Golden State

So, there we were, on breathtaking Four Mile Beach in California, the Golden State just outside Santa Cruz, on a beautiful, sun-filled afternoon in July, celebrating our first California Employee Appreciation Day with a beach party, complete with barbecue, volleyball, music, and relaxation.

It was three years into the Great Recession, but our California management operation was flourishing, and no one was thinking about the recession on that beautiful summer day. A group of the guys were grilling skirt steak for burritos, wonderful aromas were wafting through the air, and other folks were engaged in a semi-competitive volleyball game, yelling at "made" and "missed" shots, while I entertained myself and others playing a variety of Jimmy Buffett songs and others on my Larrivee acoustic guitar, as I've done in an amateur fashion for decades.

Yes, there we were again, in a market we had never planned on entering, enjoying the fruits of our labor on a path we had never expected to pursue. And here's what led up to that.

It began less than a year into the Great Recession, and we were actively, or perhaps desperately, seeking new business to replace our losses. The Phoenix economy had tanked, losing over 297,000 jobs since September 2008, and with apartment occupancies and income plummeting, our business had declined precipitously.

In a fortunate break for us, it was at that low point that we were referred to a potential client by the same broker who had referred us to the "client previously introduced in 'Satan Knocking'" the year before, but this time the potential client was a much more reputable apartment owner and one we felt would be a good addition to our client base. So we actively courted this owner and his lead asset manager, as we were vying for the management of a 150-unit apartment community they owned in Phoenix just west of the Scottsdale border. The property was performing horribly, and they were losing more money each month.

We started with introductory phone discussions, followed by their making a trip from their offices in San Jose, California, to see some of the properties we managed and spend time with us in person to get to know us better and talk about the potential management of their property. Well, long story short, we hit it off rather well, and within a couple of weeks, after several discussions, they made the decision to retain us to manage their property. And we were off.

They were hiring us to "turn their property around." In our business, we refer to "turning around" an underperforming property as improving its overall management by increasing occupancy and rent collections, improving the overall appearance of the property, improving resident relations, completing outstanding work orders on apartments that had been requested, and sometimes lowering or "containing" expenses in cases where the prior management company was spending money needlessly. When combined, these improvements to operations result in "turning around performance" and increasing bottom-line income, which is the goal of any apartment owner/landlord. And we were proven experts in turning around underperforming properties.

For the reader's benefit, I'd like to explain a little more about our business, that is, the apartment business. Each apartment property is its own standalone business. It is usually held as an individual company (i.e., a partnership, LLC, or corporation), and it acts as a company. It generates revenue (e.g., rent), incurs expenses (e.g., utilities, real estate taxes, maintenance costs, insurance, payroll, etc.), and it usually has a mortgage to pay with dollars remaining after expenses are paid. Dollars remaining after the mortgage is paid is "income" to the owner/landlord. In other businesses, it might be called a "profit." This particular property, which we had just started managing, had been purchased by the owner/client a few years before for a price of around $8,500,000, and he had placed a mortgage on the property of around $6,000,000, so he had invested approximately $2,500,000 of his own money to buy it. It was, therefore, a significant investment.

So, when occupancy declined early on in the Great Recession, and his expenses increased due to floundering management, he was losing money each month after paying the mortgage and expenses. Clearly, this was not what he'd intended when he'd initially invested in the property; thus, he needed it "turned around."

Now, turning around a large apartment property is not an overnight proposition, no matter how good you are at implementing good management. Rents are collected on a monthly basis, so increasing occupancy through new renters only impacts bottom-line income after thirty days. In other words, if you rent an apartment on June 15 for a move-in date of July 1, the income will not impact this month (i.e., June) at all, while expenses will eat up the income that is coming in.

And when you take over the management of a poorly performing property, it's usually poorly maintained as well, and thus it presents itself poorly to potential renters, who will then choose to rent elsewhere. So, you need to spend some time cleaning and spiffing it up in order to attract renters, and you need time to start up a marketing outreach program to attract those potential new renters to come see the newly spiffed-up apartment community. This takes time, all in all, anywhere from a couple weeks to one, two, or three months or more to move occupancy upward and show significant improvement in income… that is, to "turn the property around." And that's what we do.

So we got to it. We swept the parking lots, planted flowers, trimmed the trees, decorated model apartments, freshened up the rental office, repainted the signs, and overall, made the property look like new. We designed and launched a new property website, distributed five thousand marketing fliers to nearby businesses whose employees were our target renters, and placed an experienced rental manager on the property who had worked with us on other properties. And property performance started turning around. Occupancy increased as we rented apartments, income increased accordingly with our more experienced manager running things on-site, expenses were contained (i.e., decreased), and before long, the bottom-line income increased to a more favorable level. All in all, it took about ninety days to get occupancy up, and another sixty days to "stabilize income," but we had done it—we had turned it around.

And that's where California came in. We hadn't known of the owner's properties in California, but after succeeding with his Phoenix properties, he approached us for discussion. We learned he had more than twenty properties in the vicinity of San Jose and the smaller beach towns south to Monterey Bay, and he needed help, as they were generally underperforming. Wow, we had never considered California, and although we'd spent a fair amount of time there on vacations, we had never been to this area before. And that's when we heard His *whisper*. Here was a golden opportunity (no pun intended) that came out of nowhere, with a client we liked working with, and He was prodding us. So, of course, we accepted the assignments, and soon thereafter, we started up operations in California, the Golden State.

Well, as you've probably guessed, we were quite successful in "turning those properties around," as well. Our client loved us, and after a year of successful operations, he offered to host our first California

Employee Appreciation Day with a party at the beach. And so we had our party. With expansion into California as well as Texas, ParaWest was on its feet again, despite the fact that the Great Recession still had the Phoenix economy on its knees. Opportunities had come from places we hadn't expected and led to opportunities we never would have looked for, all because He knew, and He whispered.

GOD NOTE

There but for the Grace of God

My first thought when Delane told me about the phone call was "No... Hands down, no way."

The call had come from a relative, a family member, one with whom we had been close in the past but not so much in recent years. She was calling to ask for help, Delane explained. She had made a mistake, a big one, and she needed help to afford legal assistance to avoid really bad consequences. So, of course, my first thought, as usual, was, "No... Hands down, no way." But that wasn't the end of it.

Our family member had, indeed, made a "big" mistake, but she was a good person, a loving person, and a kind person, who had made a bad decision and gotten into trouble. And she was family.

The call and request came not too long after we had started ParaWest, and while we were doing okay financially, we certainly weren't well off. But immediately after my initial negative thought, I heard His *whisper: Maybe you are being too hasty in your judgment.* And wasn't there something in the Bible about helping family? The thought and vague recollection nagged at me. So I looked it up, and there it was:

> *But if anyone does not provide for his relatives, and especially for members of his household, he has denied the faith and is worse than an unbeliever.*
>
> — 1 Timothy 5:8 ESV

So, there was my answer. And yes, we loaned her the money, which helped keep her out of jail, but not without some pretty severe other consequences imposed by the court. But at least she was able to get on with her life. Two years later, she paid us back, and her life was on a sound footing. She didn't make the same mistake again.

This was only the first of many instances after starting ParaWest when we've been asked to help family, friends, and employees. And while we are careful to be prudent in offering assistance, we are not reluctant to do so. We understand that this world is often not fair, that people face hardships; trying times; and health, financial, and other problems, and it's not necessarily their fault. Everyone needs a leg up once in a while. Helping is one of the responsibilities God imposes on us, not as a quid pro quo for His blessings, but rather because it is the Christian and loving thing to do.

So, despite my initial negative reaction, one that to this day often still occurs when someone asks for help, His *whisper* will typically get the better of me, and we'll be there for them and with them—without judgment and without strings.

After all, I remember what my mother always used to say: "There but for the grace of God go I."

CHAPTER 17

The Rising Sun

It was 2011, and ParaWest was on its way again. We had recovered from the Great Recession and were growing in multiple markets. It was a somewhat jubilant time, kind of like when Old Testament folks recovered from famine or plagues. It felt good, and yes, it had really felt "that bad" along the way. And here's what led up to that.

According to economists, the Great Recession ended in 2011, three and a half years after it began. By that time, ParaWest had effectively recovered as well, having replaced the business it lost early in the recession with new business in new markets. For others, the effects of the recession lasted much longer. Overall, employment in the United States took six and a half years to fully return to pre-recession levels, and nineteen months longer for the Phoenix metro area. Between October 2008 and April 2009, seven hundred thousand jobs were lost each month, and by 2010, it was estimated that almost nine million jobs had been lost. Homelessness increased exponentially, and by mid-2009, there were nearly seven hundred thousand people homeless in the United States, living on the streets and under overpasses. Families living below the poverty level increased by an astounding 20 percent, and suicides resulting from economic influences skyrocketed. Yes, without a doubt, this had been the worst economic disaster in almost eighty years.

ParaWest's portfolio of managed properties declined from twenty-three total properties, managed in June of 2007, to thirteen by June of 2009, and our unit count—that is, the number of apartments managed—declined from 2,390 to 1,008. Our Arizona properties were impacted at a significantly higher rate, declining from twenty-one properties in 2007 to six in 2009, a 71 percent decline. Our income plummeted, and our thus-far successful entrepreneurial venture, ParaWest, had been in jeopardy.

But the sun rose again, and by June 2011, ParaWest's portfolio had grown to thirty-seven total properties, divided between Arizona, Texas, and California, which had smaller properties and units per property. We had returned to 90 percent of our pre-recession level of total units, and our income had returned. Texas and California had been ParaWest's salvation in getting through the recession and moving us into the future. Houston, particularly, would prove to be our revenue generator moving into the future. With its large and growing economy and its soaring job creation, Houston would be the kind of apartment market that would fuel our growth for years to come.

It had been an arduous road, though, and at our lowest point in 2009, we were seriously concerned. But God had lit our path. He led us into opportunistic markets we had never considered, and to clients that would provide stability for our company long into the future. Yes, instead of giving up, we had listened to His *whispers*, buckled down, and worked harder than ever, and as our business recovered, it was clear that His *whispers*, His direction, and His faithfulness had seen us through all along the way.

Refugees from Myanmar (formerly known as Burma)
at Thanksgiving buffet

Thanksgiving prayer

Thanksgiving piñata

Newly immigrated Myanmar refugee girl enjoying
Thanksgiving

God Whispers Are Life Changers

Grandaddy Nile crocodile on the Zambezi River in southeast
Zambia

Elephant herd along the Zambezi River

Hippos along the Zambezi River

Adult baboon on the walkway to Victoria Falls

God Whispers Are Life Changers

Zebras near Victoria Falls

Celebration at Kabwata Orphanage with author entertaining
the kids

Kids playing at Kabwata Orphanage

Kids from Kabwata Orphanage shown in front of their
schoolhouse

God Whispers Are Life Changers

Dining room at the orphanage

PART III
Deliverance

CHAPTER 18

Kissing Frogs

A s we began our tenth year, things were going well for ParaWest. The recession was behind for us, but not for all Americans, many of whom had lost homes or businesses to foreclosure or bankruptcy along the way. And one of those individuals who had fared poorly through that time was our former client and partner. Yes, the same one who had taken us to Houston to begin with. When all was said and done, he had gone out of the apartment business entirely and moved on.

His legacy with ParaWest, however, lived on, creating opportunities that would take us into the future, and we knew God had placed him in our path. You see, because he had invited us to partner with him on our first apartment acquisition, we had a start—a track record, if you will, albeit a small one—that would enable us to move forward with other acquisitions in the future. While apartment management would always be our foundation and our "bread and butter," so to speak, ownership interests in properties would provide a secondary revenue source and an attractive one, and lead to a "new chapter" for ParaWest. So, two years later, we sold our first apartment property we had been able to acquire as we came out of the recession, and here's what led up to that.

We began in 2011 by developing presentation materials to use while meeting with potential investors/partners. We networked with nearly everyone we had ever done business with. You see, we not only had to find partners who would invest large amounts of money into deals, but we needed a different partner, one who had the net worth and creditworthiness to qualify for a multimillion-dollar loan. All in all, it was a tough row to hoe.

As we networked, a friend—who was also a Harvard scholar—told me, "You've got to kiss a lot of frogs to find a prince," meaning, of course, that we would need to reach out to many people before we likely would find an appropriate partner. He was right. It took us nearly a year of networking, calling, meeting, and presenting until we finally found our partner. The fit was good, and we had heard His *whisper* as we met with our new partner and started forward.

So we were after our first (on our own) apartment deal. Now, sourcing apartment properties to buy was something in which we had extensive experience, as we had been doing it for our clients for more than a decade. So, when we struck out to find our own deal, we knew what we were doing. Within a short time, we had located a 362-unit apartment community built in 1968 in a great location near the Galleria Shopping Mall in Houston, Texas. We were able to place the property under contract to purchase without much problem, but then things started to stall.

As I explained, we needed both a partner to qualify for our loan, which we had, but we now needed a partner/investor to put up $5.5 million—and that we didn't yet have. You see, we couldn't secure a partner for this investment until we had the actual property under contract to purchase. So, it was kind of like the "chicken and the egg" scenario, and we had to find a property so we could then seek out an investor. And that's what we did.

We had a sixty-day window in which to find and secure our investor/partner or we'd have to terminate the purchase contract, at which point we'd have lost a significant amount of money that had been spent on legal fees, appraisals, engineering reports, and so forth. So, during that sixty-day window, we networked with every potential investor and investment broker we knew. With all that, we were still coming up short as our window began to close, at forty days out, fifty days out… and then there came a *whisper*.

Out of almost nowhere, an investment broker to whom we had been introduced by our former client and partner came to us with a potential investor. But our time was short, and we couldn't prolong the process if the investor was to take his time in touring the property, reviewing the books and records, etc. We were on a short fuse. But it happened. It turned out the potential investor was a billionaire banker with a staff of hundreds, and he could complete the property review in no time at all; he could then "write a check" without delay. And that's what he did. We closed escrow and bought the apartment property. God had led us through!

Well, we renovated that property inside and out, with new flooring, lighting, plumbing, carpentry fixtures, and much more on the apartment interiors, as well as new siding, roofing, parking lots, and swimming pools on the outside, and lastly, we redecorated and furnished the office and clubhouse. Renters loved the new look, and occupancy ran high. Two years later, we were able to sell the property, which resulted in a nice profit for our investor and a great "success story" to add to ParaWest's track record as we looked to acquire other properties going forward.

We were also able to pay a generous referral fee to our former client and partner as our way of recognizing his initial generosity and thanking him for taking us to Houston and inviting us to partner with him along the way. Yes, this was the start of a wonderful new chapter for ParaWest that He had opened for us, as we closed the book on the worst recession of the past seventy years and moved on.

GOD NOTE

Through All Those Years

One of God's strongest *whispers* over the course of our entrepreneurial adventure seemingly came out of nowhere and would impact ParaWest's business for many years. It came about when we were "kissing a lot of frogs," seeking a partner/investor with net worth and creditworthiness to qualify for multimillion-dollar loans on apartment acquisitions. Yes, we were networking with everyone we knew during that year. Along the way, we had gotten a lot of leads on potential partners from time to time, but nothing had panned out.

Well, as He would have it, one day I was speaking to my friend, the CEO of the international charity that includes Bread and Water for Africa, just generally catching up on things. My friend was telling me about the projects he was working on, and I was telling him about mine, including our search for a potential partner. Now, we had stayed in touch, and we spoke every so often, often talking about both our African involvement and plans, as well as other general business, and on that particular day, we were just shooting the breeze like always.

It all changed, however, when I mentioned our search, and immediately, without hesitation, my friend replied, "We might want to do that." Wow, what a *whisper*! "What do you mean?" I asked. I didn't know much about the overall scope of his organization, only that it included the Affordable Housing Division, as well as Bread and Water for Africa, with which we were by then well acquainted.

It turns out, however, that they had significant capital reserves accumulated from years of successful investments, primarily from their affordable housing apartment communities. And he explained it would benefit their organization by diversifying into the type of apartment investments we were proposing, which would generate additional funds that would go back into their reserves for use in funding their numerous charitable works in the United States and around the world.

In order for our apartment communities to qualify for their "affordable housing" investment, however, the property rents would have to meet certain affordability requirements using formulas developed by HUD, and the properties would also have to provide resident services, such as back-to-school supplies, summer meals for kids, and others. Well, our "workforce"-level apartments fit those requirements perfectly. Our renter profile was generally blue-collar and entry-level white-collar workers, and all our properties had resident programs because that was close to our hearts and had been part of our approach from the beginning. So, the fit was there. And so we moved forward as partners, and for the next many years, we would acquire, renovate, and sell numerous apartment properties together, generating funds for the charity and business opportunities for ParaWest.

All of this took place because God had led us through all those years, which had started back in 1995, when Delane and I worked together at another company and first met our later-to-become friend, the president of an international charity, as he retained us to manage their affordable housing apartments in Phoenix, Arizona. After having gone our separate ways at the end of the 1990s, we had then reached out to him during the early years of ParaWest to inquire about and begin our involvement in the charity's work in sub-Saharan Africa. And then several years after that, as we were beginning a new chapter at ParaWest and moving forward after the Great Recession, we connected once more through that chance phone call and found common ground for working together. Coincidences? Fate? No, it was Him all along.

Author's Note:

Throughout this book, I'll refer to this partner as our "financial partner," as they were able to bring to our partnership the net worth and creditworthiness needed to obtain large loans. Our other partners in transactions, referred to as "investment partners," were able to invest significant amounts of equity in transactions to meet our equity requirements. *Equity* refers to the investment dollars put up by an investment group (usually 25 to 30 percent of the total cost), which when added to the funds obtained from a mortgage loan, equal the total dollars invested in a property.

CHAPTER 19
A Silver Lining

It was 2013, and the Great Recession was in our rearview mirror. With a new year about to start, we were joyful and hopeful. That joy and hope, however, was soon to be shattered—almost. And here's what led up to that.

On January 2, we got the call. We were in the Orlando airport on a layover, waiting for our final flight home to Phoenix, when it came. It was Kim calling from our Houston office. "We've had a fire," she said. "Twenty-four apartments were destroyed at our property in Westchase. Thankfully, no one was hurt."

"How'd it start?" I asked.

"Seems a young woman in her twenties had her first real Christmas tree and didn't know that you have to keep water in the stand to keep the tree from drying out. Her dried-out tree was easily ignited, by what we don't know, and it went up like charcoal starter. Spread so fast the fire department couldn't contain it before it had destroyed the entire building, twenty-four apartments."

Now, fires are scary things. They can destroy the personal possessions of a lifetime. They can hurt people. They can kill people. And when you "manage" an apartment community, it becomes your responsibility. You may have had nothing to do with it, but it is still your responsibility. The apartment residents living there are your responsibility, and if the fire was caused by something a maintenance technician did wrong, such as an incorrectly wired light fixture, it can be catastrophic in terms of financial repercussions for negligence.

So, even though ParaWest bore no fault in this fire occurring, it was still our responsibility to take care of the displaced residents—to find them new or temporary homes and help them through the night with food and clothing while arranging for their housing. Additionally, there were huge potential financial implications. Although apartment communities are insured, insurance doesn't always cover the full cost of lost income and sometimes other indirect costs, such as putting up displaced residents in hotels and providing other support to help get them through. Yes, fires are scary, and they have huge potential ramifications.

It was a devastating start to the new year, and all kinds of anxious thoughts went through my mind. This fire was particularly worrisome because we had the property under contract for sale, and I thought that now that might fall through. This sale falling through would be particularly impactful to our business because Delane and I had ownership interest in the property and were therefore invested in the sale. Wow, what a blow!

We had acquired this property four years before through a partnership with our client who had originally taken us to Houston just prior to the Great Recession. As the Great Recession struck, however, our business plan for the property was never fully realized as it was difficult to maintain occupancy, and many residents who lost jobs were unable to pay their rent, creating bad debt writeoffs and resulting in reduced income for the property. We managed to squeak through, however, and when the economy and apartment market started to improve, we decided our best course of action was to sell the property, which would provide a modest return to our investors, and we could move on to other opportunities. So we moved forward and placed the property under contract with a buyer.

We were moving through the sales process with the buyer reviewing all the property records, conducting inspections, and working to place financing on the property—and then this fire happened. *Up in smoke*, I thought. But I was wrong. My greatest worries never came to pass. God had whispered that we would be okay, and as things played out, we were.

We immediately contacted the buyer to disclose the fire and its impact, and at the same time, we reached out to our insurance company and filed a claim. Well, lo and behold, the buyer decided to move forward with the transaction as long as the building would be rebuilt and paid for with the insurance proceeds. The insurance company was more than accommodating, advancing funds to cover lost rent and the relocation of residents, and after inspections and estimates by contractors, they covered the full cost of reconstruction.

So there we were with our silver lining. You see, the end result of that fire was not devastation to our business, but rather a bonus to the buyer, who ended up with twenty-four "new" apartments in the 1980s-built, "vintage" property they purchased. Now new units command higher rents than thirty-year-old ones, and the higher rents result in higher value. So, we got our sale completed, and our buyer got a bonus.

As an additional blessing from this whole nerve-racking event, ParaWest established an emergency team to respond to events such as fires, hurricanes, and other potential disasters. The team is composed of regional managers, experienced site managers, and supervisory and assistant maintenance technicians. Members of this team are on call 24/7, and they can respond to an event on a moment's notice. Their purpose is to manage the situation by working with residents, securing damaged sites for security and safety reasons, coordinating with any first responders, working with the Red Cross to provide temporary food and shelter, and generally to make sure everything is handled for the benefit of impacted residents on our properties. Over the years, this team has been called on to respond to other fires, hurricanes, and floods, positively impacting the lives of hundreds of residents who have found themselves in one of these unfortunate situations.

We were clearly in God's hands on that fateful day in early January, when a young woman's negligence could have had devastating effects on so many, but didn't, and instead it resulted in a silver lining in the months to follow, as well as the years after that.

CHAPTER 20

Teach a Man to Fish

Today, Kabwata Orphanage's fish farm produces hundreds of pounds of tilapia each year, providing a diet of protein to the kids who live there, as well as supplemental income to help support the orphanage through sales to local markets and restaurants. The fish are raised in three large, man-made ponds that have been constructed in various phases over the past several years, on land owned by the orphanage's founder, Angela Miyanda. The fish farm is an incredibly successful program for Kabwata, but it took a lot of work to get there. It had its mustard-seed roots from another continent half a world away, it suffered from some false starts at the beginning, and then, over time, it evolved to produce the high harvest levels it currently achieves, and here's what led up to that.

We were coming out of the Great Recession, and Delane and I were working in Phoenix with a charitable ministry called Mentor Kids, USA, also known as MK. The ministry had originally started out as a one-on-one mentoring program that partnered an adult with an underprivileged, and in most cases, single-parent, elementary school–aged child or a young teenager, in order to help them gain self-esteem and learn life skills along the way. MK had recently redirected its program from the one-on-one focus to serving "Promise Neighborhoods." Promise Neighborhoods were located in lower-income areas of Phoenix, Arizona, and MK would start up after-school programs for the underprivileged kids living there to help them with their academics, self-esteem, and social skills, as well as introduce them to a relationship with God (but more on that later).

Anyway, MK had a Promise Neighborhood in a poverty-stricken area of South Phoenix, where they had been working with a local church in providing programs for the neighborhood kids for a few years at that point. The leaders wanted to help the program become more self-sufficient financially, and they had come up with the idea of raising fish in a "swimming pool" and selling them to local restaurants to raise funds. They felt this could be a good program for the kids to get involved with helping to feed and care for the fish, and to participate in the proceeds—the "fruit of their labors." They already had several small community gardens and were able to sell their produce to local restaurants, so this seemed like a natural extension of that good work.

And so they began. They purchased and installed an above-ground swimming pool, fitted it with appropriate filter and circulating pump equipment, and started with their first batch of fingerling tilapia. And that's when things went south. You see, in a city like Phoenix, or probably in any American city, the City Health Department has a myriad of rules and regulations that preclude you from starting a small neighborhood fish farm like this. Without going into all the ins and outs, suffice it to say that before the fish farm ever got off the ground, it was done, closed down, finished.

But God had another plan. You see, I had learned of the fish farm, and in those early days of working with Bread and Water for Africa, I had frequently been in contact with its director, Beth, about various ideas and programs we might implement to help Kabwata. Well, I'm not even sure how this took root, but somewhere along the way, I explained to Beth about the failed fish farm, and she, in turn, took the idea and passed it along to Angela at Kabwata, and it grew from there.

It wasn't as simple as that, however. When Angela initially built Kabwata's first pond and tried to raise tilapia, the effort failed. Yes, dead fish and all, it hadn't worked out. And that's when God stepped in. Angela got referred to the Zambian Ministry of Fisheries and Livestock, a department of the Zambian government, which, in turn, assigned an expert in fish farming to assist her in her efforts. This turned out to be the expertise she needed, and with this assistance, she was able to construct her initial tilapia pond, and later a second, and then a third, until Kabwata's successful fish farming program was underway.

The ponds were initially dug out in a field, each one a little over an acre in size with a depth of four feet. The dug-out retention area has a liner made of high-density polyethylene plastic to enable it to hold water without seepage. A nearby irrigation well is needed to provide water, and then the ponds are filled and ready for fingerlings. Fingerling tilapia start out only one to two inches long, and they grow to about ten inches. The fingerlings are introduced into the ponds, where they are fed for six to nine months before being harvested. The ponds are designed to specific measurements so workers can stand in the water from one side all the way to the opposite side and drag nets through the pond to harvest the mature fish. It takes six to ten men to man the net and drag it from one end of the pond to the other to secure the harvest. By cultivating three one-acre ponds, Kabwata is able to stagger the planting and cultivating of the tilapia so they can provide fish for both the kids and for marketing throughout the entire year.

For years, the kids at Kabwata Orphanage had little protein in their diets, as meat prices were much too high for them to afford. With the harvest from their fish ponds, however, they have been able to enjoy protein-rich fish in their diet every week, a highly prized improvement, indeed. And when combined with the benefit of the additional revenue provided by selling the surplus fish to local restaurants, Kabwata's fish farm has become one of its most successful ventures on the road to self-sufficiency. It is a remarkable endeavor, one that started with a *whisper* halfway around the world in a modest neighborhood in south Phoenix, Arizona, then developed into a production program that provides fish to feed the children of Kabwata Orphanage for a lifetime.

CHAPTER 21

Organic Growth

ParaWest grew rapidly during the years following the recession through both external new growth and internal "organic growth." New growth included taking on new clients, establishing relationships, and managing these new properties as they came on board. Organic growth came from two main sources. The first was our participation in ownership interests in acquiring new properties, which we would then manage and renovate. The second source came from our existing client base as they bought more apartment properties, which we would then manage, and in most cases, renovate, as well.

Now, I don't believe that the scholarly economists who coined the term *organic growth* in business realized that in order to be organic, something must be natural—that is, it must come from God. But it does. And it did for ParaWest and for Delane and me. It was an upbeat time at ParaWest, and with the benefit of this organic growth expanding our business, we were able to expand our involvement with the ministries we served, as well. So, over the next few years, our portfolio of managed properties increased significantly, as did our ministry outreach, and here's what led up to that.

Following our first apartment property acquisition with our new financial partner, we were able to quickly complete another transaction with a different investment partner the following year. After that, however, things slowed for a while. We had stalled along the way and hadn't been able to complete another transaction after working to put something together for nearly a year. And that's when it came: the *whisper*. You see, out of the blue we received a call from the investment partner who had brought that billionaire investor into our first acquisition, and he wanted us to partner with him on a new acquisition on which his company was working, a 357-unit affordable housing apartment community in Dallas, Texas. Wow, what an opportunity—and right in our wheelhouse, with an affordable housing component, as well!

Coming from an existing partner, this opportunity enabled us to acquire both an ownership interest and the management and renovation contracts, a home run in our world, so we agreed. We brought in our financial partner, as well, and we moved forward on the transaction and then the renovation and management. We quickly realized that this kind of organic growth was much more efficient than many other avenues in expanding our business, since this investment partner had done the lions' share of the front-end work in finding and securing the new property, placing the mortgage loan, and raising the investment capital for equity. And then, as He had led us through His *whisper* to this great opportunity, we were able to step in and renovate and manage the property, increasing our management portfolio along the way.

Well, the organic growth didn't stop there. Over the following two years, this same investment partner brought us four more apartment communities, comprising more than one thousand apartment units to renovate, manage, and participate in ownership. But the real blessing we received through this organic growth was one we had not expected, one we had not seen coming—because the real blessing of this kind of growth was a greater efficiency, an efficiency that provided Delane and me with more time to spend on the ministries we served, creating a sort of organic growth in that arena, as well. So, we used that time to its utmost, and here are some of the results that came about.

For Kabwata Orphanage, we spent time with Beth, director of Bread and Water for Africa (BWA), learning the needs of the children and the villagers. We worked on agricultural opportunities, including starting a banana crop—a cash crop for Kabwata, as the harvest could be sold to local markets and consumers. We started a "microloan" program (but more on that later). We helped fund construction of a hospital in Cameroon, and the completion of a medical clinic with its own water well in the rural area serving the villages outside of Lusaka. We helped hire teachers for the rural school in those same villages, distributed Bibles to the kids and others in Africa, and started a Christmas program, bringing Christmas to the kids of Kabwata Orphanage.

On the domestic front, we solidified our relationship with Mentor Kids USA (MK), assisting with Christmas and summer camp transportation, worked with their Promise Neighborhood in South Phoenix, and initiated the beginnings of a summer program for the underprivileged kids who lived in MK's newly adopted Palomino Promise Neighborhood in northeast Phoenix (and more on that later).

Those years of organic growth were, indeed, bountiful as ParaWest grew, and our ministry outreach was able to blossom. Yes, organic growth was growth that we had not expected, and it came from opportunities we had not seen coming, but He had. He had known all along!

CHAPTER 22

The Second Lady of Zambia

What would life be like if you were born into this world and abandoned? To have no bed to sleep in, no home to live in, no parents to love you, no family to fall back on? To live on the streets from early childhood into adulthood, begging for handouts, scrounging for your next meal? Living a life of hunger and despair, with no hope and no future? Most of us who have lived in America or other advanced nations all our lives can never truly imagine what it would be like. For the 1.2 million orphans in Zambia, however, and millions more living in other African countries, this is, indeed, their plight.

But one woman stood up to their plight, using her God-given abilities and resources to help. She has made a difference, and for every child who has crossed her path, she has given them a better life, a life filled with love, a life filled with meaning, and a life filled with promise and hope.

It was April 2017, and Angela Miyanda was being recognized at a celebration in her honor. It was the twentieth anniversary of the orphanage she had started, supported, and run through all those years. The room was filled with Zambian and Lusaka dignitaries, as well as representatives of Bread and Water for Africa—Delane and me—who had traveled nine thousand miles from Arizona to attend. There were also several adults who had grown up at Kabwata Orphanage, and now they were living productive and fruitful lives; they were there to tell their stories.

Yes, Angela had given her time, her efforts, and her blood, sweat, and tears over the past twenty years to this God-led endeavor. Over that time, more than 550 children had called Kabwata Orphanage their home, many of whom have since grown up and gone on to successful careers and families as adults, while others have arrived there more recently and are just beginning their lives as toddlers or young children at the orphanage. Yes, Angela was, indeed, deserving of this recognition. It was a glorious celebration, and here's what led up to that.

"I woke up one day, it was in the nineties, and I said to my husband, 'I need to start an orphanage,'" was how Angela Miyanda explained it to me on my first trip to Zambia in 2008, when I asked her how it had all started. It was that simple.

This story, however, really wasn't simple at all!

It was 1997 when Angela woke up to her epiphany. She was the "Second Lady" of Zambia. Her husband, former brigadier-general Godfrey Miyanda, was the vice president, having held the office since 1993. Yes, this was no ordinary woman making this statement on that morning in 1997, and her husband, to whom she expressed her desire, was no ordinary husband. Together they had risen to political heights in this relatively new, democratic country, formerly known as Northern Rhodesia, which had only won its independence from the United Kingdom three decades before.

Angela had been the Second Lady for almost four years, and during that time, she had seen firsthand the devastation wrought by AIDS, as well as its impact on families and on the children of her home country. Zambia had, at the time, one of the highest proportions of orphaned children in the world, and it had resulted from HIV/AIDS having decimated the adult population over the years leading up to and continuing into the late 1990's. "I founded Kabwata Orphanage and Transit Centre in response to the plight of children orphaned by HIV/

AIDS," Angela told Gene Krizek, the founder of Bread and Water for Africa, at the time.

And, indeed, she had. She had moved ahead with her "need to start an orphanage" just as she said she would. Angela not only provided the financial startup with the help of others, but she brought to bear her full personal efforts, working long hours every day from early to late to make her vision a reality. Shortly after her epiphany, she assembled her resources, obtained a long-term lease on a run-down former British estate property in Lusaka, and began her quest. The estate had several uninhabitable buildings, but nothing that was useable. So Angela set about building her orphanage block by block, building by building, and courtyard by courtyard, until twenty years later, the facility had two large dormitory rooms, one for boys and one for girls, housing for the "aunties" who cared for the children, a kitchen, a large dining room that could accommodate everyone, a laundry room, a library, and play areas and a garden in the back. She began taking in children soon after establishing the first buildings in the compound, and she has been doing so ever since.

Yes, Angela is truly a God-led woman whose faith is her only trait stronger than her determination. Zambia is primarily a Christian nation, and Angela is a strong Christian leader. Her faith is embedded in the orphanage in every way, from the love and security provided to the children, to their education, their music, and especially their charity toward each other, from the youngest toddler to the teenagers to the adults who grew up there and now serve. And charity to one another is not always an easy task, considering that the orphanage is home to more than sixty individuals all living together under one roof, so to speak.

Angela tells it best in her own words, as she proclaimed at Kabwata Orphanage's twentieth-anniversary celebration. "The greatest achievement we celebrate are the children who have made it and are able to fend for themselves. I have had wonderful people around… it has been a collection of so many people. It is not me and myself, but God."

Yes, Angela had heard God's *whisper* on that early morning in 1997. She had heard it, and she responded, and children's lives have been blessed for decades as a result.

CHAPTER 23

Of Bangladesh and Cameroon

In 2015, Bread and Water for Africa's ministry in Cameroon reported the following progress on their microloan program, which had been in place for the past three years:

> *Pascaline Ndilengtieh reported that the one-hundred-dollar loan she had received was used for purchasing fertilizer for her rice farming. This had increased her 'output' and she has been able to pay 'all of her debts.'" The original loan has since been repaid.*
>
> *Mary Fehnyui's one-hundred-dollar loan was used to establish a "provision store" offering "foodstuffs" in front of her house, which has become the primary source of "her livelihood." Her loan has been repaid in full.*
>
> *Vivian Mbipefah used her two-hundred-dollar loan to expand her product sales from fish to also include corn and beans. The added income helped her to provide for her "family's livelihood." Her loan has been repaid.*

While these may seem like small success stories, in the lives of these widows living in poverty in Bamenda and Bangolan Cameroon, the small loans made the difference between hunger and health for their families and provided purpose and self-esteem for the women themselves. But these are only a few examples, as the program has touched the lives of many more individuals over the few years it has been in effect, and here's what led up to that.

Back during the recession, Delane and I first learned about "microloans" through reading about their origins, opportunities, and implementation. Microloans are "very small loans" made to impoverished borrowers to support entrepreneurship and alleviate poverty. Some say the concept dates back to John Wesley, the leader of the reform movement against the Church of England and the founder of the Methodist Church, who wrote of it in his journal in 1746:

> *I made a public collection toward a lending stock for the poor. Our rule is, to lend only twenty shillings at once ($140 in today's currency), which is repaid weekly within three months.... Out of this, no less than two hundred and fifty-five persons have been relieved (helped) in eighteen months.*

In the modern era, however, the concept originated in Bangladesh, a small country located just west of Myanmar in Southeast Asia. Bangladesh is an extremely impoverished country, and in 2009, a UNICEF report found that thirty-three million of its children, around 56 percent, were living below the International Poverty Line, defined as disposable income of one dollar per person per day in U.S. dollars. The concept was the creation of Muhammad Yunus, a professor at the University of Chittagong, who, in 1976, began his microloan project in a small town in Bangladesh called Jobra using his own money.

The project was so successful that in 1983, he went on to found Grameen Bank for the sole purpose of providing loans to the poorest of the poor, borrowers with no collateral to secure a loan. For his efforts and ingenuity, Professor Yunus was awarded the Nobel Peace Prize in 2006.

It has been determined that many impoverished individuals have the motivation and work ethic to succeed if provided with the opportunity. And in many third-world countries, it doesn't take a lot of money to get a small business off the ground, or to improve an already-existing small operation, such as farming. And so the microloan program began, and it has flourished ever since. As of 2009, it was reported that an estimated seventy-four million people held microloans that totaled a staggering thirty-eight billion dollars. In that same year, Grameen Bank reported an astounding repayment success rate of between 95 and 98 percent!

As we read about all of this, we heard that *whisper* loud and clear. And as I had mentioned, we had frequent discussions with Beth, the director of BWA during those years, so in one such discussion we brought up the microloan project. You see, it requires relatively modest funding; you can start a program with anywhere from a few hundred to a few thousand dollars. And so we did. In talking with Beth about Zambia, however, we determined that Angela had too much going on, what with the orphanage itself, the new banana crop, and the fish farm. But Beth had another idea. It seemed BWA's ministry in Cameroon involved a number of widows, determined women who were heads of households and who tried their best, but they had a tough time making ends meet in providing for their families.

So with His *whisper* in our hearts, Delane and I decided to start this venture in Cameroon. Located just north of the equator in central Africa with a coastline on the Atlantic Ocean, Cameroon is a severely impoverished nation where 57 percent of the population lives below the international poverty level. Living conditions are poor, crime is rampant, and with the government being "rife with corruption," according to numerous public policy reports, the success of any business or economic endeavor is difficult.

BWA was already working with a ministry in Cameroon, so they had an administrator for the program, their so-called boots on the ground. And upon further inquiry, we determined that there were groups of women, widows mostly, who worked at or ran small businesses and would be the perfect benefactors of a microloan program. So we began our first microloan program, and this whispered idea went from seedling to full-blown implementation in only a few months, a pretty amazing feat in sub-Saharan Africa, where things typically move slowly.

So the program was up and running. We had started with a two-thousand-dollar fund the first year, increasing it to three thousand the second year, and four thousand the third. Part of the increase came from the modest interest (i.e., 3 percent) that was earned. The program was designed so that the interest earned, combined with the repayment of loans in a relatively short period of time, resulted in a microloan program that was designed to be not only self-sustaining, but actually able to grow over time. What a success! Lives were being changed. Children were being blessed. Loans were being repaid. All this from a new idea we had "stumbled" onto as we opened our eyes, ears, and hearts to His *whisper*. He hasn't disappointed!

CHAPTER 24

They Come and They Go

There's an axiom in our business that goes something like this: "At the end of the day, all management accounts will eventually go away."

Now, this axiom probably applies to any business. In service businesses, contracts come and go. In retail, product lines go in and out of favor, and therefore, they come and go. In restaurants, tastes and social behaviors change and come and go, and the list could go on and on. Just change the type of business, and it'll fit.

In apartment management, there are a few reasons for this, including the following:

1. If you do a really good job, the apartment property goes up in value, and the owner will sell to realize his profit.
2. You might do a really good job and make it look too easy, and because an owner doesn't see all the myriads of customer interactions and "behind the scenes" workings of management, they decide to take over the management on their own, which usually doesn't work out, but that's not relevant here.
3. On the other hand, if you don't do a good enough job, or market or economic circumstances result in your achieving less-than-optimal results, an owner may elect

to change to another management company with the hopes that they'll do better.

4. And finally, in the end, if you manage a property long enough, an owner may go on to "meet his Maker," in which case his estate, including the apartment properties, will be passed on to someone else, who may have different ideas, directions, or objectives, in which case you'll end up out of the job along the way.

So, one way or the other, they come and they go.

But there's another more unusual reason for a management account going away. Yes, it happened to ParaWest, and here's what led up to that.

As I explained earlier, we experienced wonderful organic growth through an investment partner who brought us several management accounts over a three-year period. We had a great relationship, and the properties were operating successfully in generating cash flow for our partner.

Our relationship over this time was primarily with the company's director of investments, although there were two principals who actually owned the company, and he reported to them. We had, of course, met these principals and developed a relatively positive relationship, as well, but our main contact and our day-to-day business was conducted with the director. Well, after three years of working together, out of the blue, the director met with us in Dallas one afternoon and explained that he was leaving this company, our investment partner, and starting his own firm.

Now, that immediately elicited thoughts circling through my mind as to whether this might be a good thing or a bad thing. First, in starting his own firm, he would be competing directly with his former company, our investment partner, probably targeting some of the same apartment properties for acquisition. Second, on the other hand, he would be retaining us to manage those properties, so we would have the benefit of additional organic growth. So, overall, it was a mixed bag as to the effect on ParaWest, and no *whispers* seemed forthcoming. Without that clear direction, we followed the easiest path and moved forward in working with his new firm while continuing to manage the properties owned by our investment partner.

We found our investment partner to be rather amenable to the change as they hired a new chief financial officer (CFO) to replace the former director of investments. We soon found ourselves reporting directly to him, and that seemed to be going well. On the other front, our new client, the former director, had moved on with his new firm in looking to acquire his first apartment properties. After several months had gone by, however, and he hadn't acquired anything, we assumed that avenue was probably not going to happen for ParaWest, but our relationship with our investment partner was still good, and we were continuing to manage all their properties for them.

Almost one year later, we got the call. It was the former director, now the owner of his new firm. We learned that he had placed two apartment properties, totaling 528 apartments, under contract to purchase in Fort Worth, Texas, and he wanted us to partner with him to manage and renovate the properties. Wow, what an opportunity! No *whispers*, though, and we continually thought about the potential negative impact of him "competing with" his former firm, our investment partner. But with no signs of such impact, we moved forward with him on the acquisition and management.

Well, things started out positively enough as we closed escrow on the properties, took over the management, and started renovations. All seemed good to go. And that's when it happened. The CFO, who was still relatively new to our investment partner's company, planned to make a trip to Scottsdale to visit our offices and meet the team. Nothing unusual about that. And so he came, and so we met. In the course of our discussions, however, he mentioned, somewhat offhandedly, that the principals of his firm weren't too pleased that we had "gone behind their backs and outbid them on the five hundred units in Fort Worth." So there it was—the hammer.

Now, we hadn't been involved in the actual acquisition of those properties since we had only gotten involved after they were already under contract to purchase. We hadn't been involved in the negotiation phase, so we had no idea as to who was bidding against whom. But that's not how it looked. And that's not how they had taken it. And despite my best efforts in explaining what had actually happened, the damage was done. Over the next six months, one by one, that former investment partner gave us thirty-day "notices to terminate" on each of our management contracts, and at the end of the day, they were all gone.

And to make matters worse, and a long story short, the former director gave us notice himself to terminate the contracts on all *his* properties eighteen months later. It seemed he had watched us do a good job; we had made it look too easy, and he had decided to manage the properties himself. So that is what he did, and then those contracts, too, were gone.

As someone once said, though, "They come, and they go." ParaWest was thriving at that time, and the impact of that lost business would be fleeting, so we weren't overly concerned. And then came the *whisper*. Yes, God had a plan for us to replace that lost business. And it would be with better business, taking us forward on an even brighter path as we moved on (but more on that later).

GOD NOTE

The Square

T he following article was originally published by the *Phoenix New Times*, a local news source.

"Gang, Bang, You're Dead"
By Michael Kiefer
September 9, 1999

Edwardo Soto knew his little brother was dead the moment he turned the corner and saw the police gathered by the ambulance. His sister Carolina was hysterical. She had called Edwardo from a pay phone and screamed that Junior had been shot.

Hector Soto Jr. was laid out on the sidewalk beneath a blue blanket. Even after his parents, Maria and Hector Sr., his cousins and a handful of close friends arrived, the police would not let them view his body until the crime-scene photographers had come and gone.

It was June 16. Carolina, 19, and Junior, 16, had been at Palomino Park, on 30th Street north of Greenway Road, in a predominantly Mexican north Phoenix neighborhood called The Square. A fight broke out between two gangs. According to some accounts, Junior ran over from the basketball court to defend a young woman he thought was Carolina. In the melee that followed, Junior took two bullets, one to the abdomen, the other to his head. He died in the back seat of his sister's car as she drove toward the hospital.

Junior had been a dignified young man, but now his family gazed on the indignity of violent death. Hector Sr. breaks down when he tries to talk about what he saw when he finally lifted the blanket.

It's an all-too-familiar story: a regular kid thoughtlessly caught up in testosterone and territoriality, the victim of adolescent impulse.

It could happen in any neighborhood. But the reality is it happens more frequently in those economically starved, politically ignored neighborhoods where street gangs have rooted like Bermuda grass. And Junior was in one of those neighborhoods.

The tragedy described in the article above happened almost ten years before Mentor Kids USA adopted Palomino as a Promise Neighborhood to help the kids and their families have a better life. But the poverty and crime that existed during that time continues today, and the neighborhood cries out—they still need our help.

Palomino has long been known as "The Square," a name that came about because the neighborhood is one mile square, and within that square mile lies an extremely impoverished and high-crime neighborhood. The name is used by the general public as well as the police and fire departments and Phoenix city government officials. It's not referred to with pride or in any positive manner; rather, it's a means to denote a neighborhood that everyone wishes they could change.

The area developed into what it became because as the city of Phoenix grew around it, with their zoning codes and city planning contributing to better housing in neighborhoods, The Square was a "county island," immune to city codes and requirements. Although the area was eventually annexed into the city of Phoenix, its development was already in place, leading to the area perpetuating a poverty lifestyle.

The families living in the neighborhood are generally very low income and predominantly Hispanic. Housing consists primarily of low-income apartment and trailer homes. The children are hindered in their educational development because of their parents' plight, which included the following challenges as identified by the Arizona Neighborhood Transformation Ministry (i.e., ATM), an international faith-based ministry:

- Parents who only speak Spanish;
- Parents with no college education and, in many cases, limited high school education;
- Parents who are unemployed or who work in very low-paying jobs; and
- Parents who work two or three jobs to survive and have very limited time to support their children's education.

Palomino Elementary School is a "Title 1" school, meaning at least 50 percent of the students' families live in poverty.

"Without educational success Palomino children will continue the cycle of poverty and health challenges, both physical and mental, that living in poverty presents," an ATM report concluded.

Crime is the other challenge families, and particularly children, must face in Palomino. Following are statistics provided by the Phoenix Police Department in their 2009 report:

- The crime level in Palomino is 250 percent higher than in surrounding neighborhoods.
- The violent crime level in Palomino is about 300 percent higher than in surrounding neighborhoods.

- Drug-related crime is five times higher in Palomino than in surrounding neighborhoods.
- And according to local resource officer (with the Phoenix Police Department) Santos Robles, there are three active gangs in the Palomino area.

And lastly, there are few safe places for the children outside of school. The following conclusions came from an ATM report in 2010:

> *While the schools and a local recreational club provide after school options for children, not all participate or are able to participate due to lack of transportation, affordability, or simply a lack of trust. Beyond these options there are really no other safe places for children to spend their time.*

Yes, Palomino is a neighborhood in need, a neighborhood crying out for help. And that's what Mentor Kids is there for—to help. To bring God's love to bear, and to make things better for the children and for the next generation. Yes, His *whisper* has been heard, and yes, we're trying.

CHAPTER 25

Swimming and STEM

It was June 2017, and fifteen first- and second-graders from Palomino in north Phoenix had just arrived in our backyard. They were talking, shouting, laughing, and giggling loudly, as little kids do, as they moved through the line covering their eyes with their hands and having their faces sprayed with sunscreen before moving on to the covered patio for breakfast. They were the first group on the first day of that year's Summer Splash Camp, and excitement was running high! The excitement was contagious for Delane and me, as well, as we greeted them with high-fives and they moved through the gate.

We were holding our third annual Mentor Kids' Summer Splash Camp, later to be renamed the Summer Enrichment Program. It had been a resounding success for the first two years. This year, some sixty elementary school–aged kids were attending the program, which was held Monday through Friday for the entire month of June. This was up from twenty-six attending the first year and forty-something the second.

Their day at camp was split between classrooms at our church, where they participated in reading, Bible studies, and STEM (Science, Technology, Engineering, and Math) classes, and our backyard, where they participated in water games and playground activities. Best of all, they learned to swim, with swimming lessons taking place each day in our backyard pool, led by an MK volunteer and certified swim instructor.

Beginning with the third year, we had added a week of Vacation Bible School (VBS) at church, a truly incredible week for kids. They were bused to and from camp each day from MK's adopted Palomino Promise Neighborhood in north Phoenix. To make it through their day at camp, they were served a nutritional breakfast and lunch, which provided the high caloric count needed by these high-energy, highly active kids. Now in its third year, this year's camp would be the best one yet, and here's what led up to that.

It was February 2015, and Delane and I were discussing how we could involve ourselves more in local ministries and reach a greater number of kids through our service. Our efforts in Africa had expanded over the past few years, and with those outreach programs reaching and blessing the kids at Kabwata, the rural villagers, and the widows in Cameroon, we wanted to turn our focus back to helping our local community, as well.

Knowing MK had expanded their local outreach through their Promise Neighborhood program, we thought our best place to start would be to reach out to them and see what we could do to get more involved, to help. In the back of our minds, always, was the wisdom of Mother Teresa: *"The poor don't need our pity or our sympathy, they need our love… they need our help!"*

So we set up a lunch meeting with our friends at MK: Chuck, the CEO; Aaron, the director of programs; and Wendy, the manager of MK's newest Promise Neighborhood, Palomino. We met on our backyard patio in February, a beautiful time of year in Scottsdale with warm sunny days, flowers blooming, and birds singing. Yes, it was just the spot to discuss God's work!

During lunch, Delane and I explained our situation and our objectives to get more involved. The MK folks updated us on the programs they had going and their plans for growth. They explained how their south Phoenix Promise Neighborhood was going well. They had established a partnership/ministry with a local church, which provided classrooms, playgrounds, a garden area, and other elements that had contributed to the program growing, and more kids were coming all the time. The program was flourishing through neighborhood resident involvement and support, combined with a hearty dose of support by the leaders of the church. The South Mountain Promise Neighborhood had an ongoing afternoon program during the school year and a summer program during the month of June. MK ran the programs with their paid manager and part-time assistant, who together coordinated everything.

Next, they explained how they had recently gotten their north Phoenix Promise Neighborhood off the ground in Palomino. They had established an afterschool program for elementary-school students. The program was run by Wendy, and more students were being added all the time. We inquired about a summer program for Palomino, and they explained they hadn't gotten that started yet. That would take planning, site location, and funding, none of which they had at that point. And there and then, on that warm sunny February day on our backyard patio, came the *whisper*.

Delane and I looked at each other knowingly, as I chimed in without a second thought, "What if we started a summer program here, in our yard? It's big, with a playground and zipline for younger kids, and a pool, a covered patio area for lunch and arts and crafts, and there's even an outdoor entrance to a bathroom off the pool for the kids to use. We could lay out blankets in shady areas for reading. And," I went on, "through the grace of God, ParaWest has had a good year, so we'd be able to cover the funding." Delane had another thought, and she added, "Let's provide swimming lessons, as well. We live in Phoenix, Arizona, where pools are more abundant than almost any other place in the country, and drownings occur far too often, with so many resulting from kids getting around pools and not knowing how to swim. Our program could save kid's lives."

So we began exploring the idea. What would it involve? Well, the MK folks knew their stuff. "We'd probably want to start with a reading program, Bible study, and arts and crafts," they offered, then went on to explain: "In a Johns Hopkins University Center for Summer Learning Study, they found that children from low-income communities lose nearly three months of grade-level equivalency during the summer months each year, compared to an average of one month lost by middle income children when reading and math performance are combined. The loss is compounded year over year for the children as they advance through grades."

"And besides the classes and the swimming," Wendy went on, "we could probably provide breakfast and lunch through the Civitan Program, which we use in south Phoenix. They deliver enough of both meals in quantities that match our count each morning. They're pre-packaged, wholesome, and nutritious, and they are provided at no cost to ministries such as ours."

So there we had it—the makings of a Summer Splash Camp for the kids from MK's Palomino Promise Neighborhood. By June, we had a full-blown program in place, complete with staff, volunteers, a swimming instructor, a daily schedule, and a chartered school bus for the month of June. And so it began. We had heard His *whisper*, and we were rolling.

But not without a few wrinkles.

GOD NOTE
His Gift

It was June the fifteenth, 2018, "Adoption Day," and we had just left Phoenix Children's Court. The adoption was done, and Roslyn was now our daughter, and we were her parents and family. What a joyous day it was! With us at court that morning were Roslyn's siblings; Scott, who lived with his father and stepmother; Oliver and Max, who were adopted on the same docket as Roslyn by a loving Christian family who were also there that day; and Coach Steve, who had run the after-school and summer kids' programs at the school Roslyn had attended for the previous three years.

We left the courtroom, all of us together, and were off to a celebratory lunch at a nearby restaurant, where we enjoyed one another's company and regaled in the joy of the day. After lunch, we called our friend Pastor Ryan, who had agreed to say a blessing for Roslyn, Delane, and me at our church, and so we headed there next. We met in the small chapel on our church campus grounds. The chapel was a small, intimate venue with a steeple on top and a large cross behind the altar, which was where we stood. It had been built only a few years before with the expansion of our church's campus. Built of stone, it was reminiscent of the smaller, humbly designed chapels of an earlier era, before larger, modern structures had been built to accommodate the ever-increasing numbers of attendees at churches such as ours. Anyway, we stood before that cross, the three of us and Pastor Ryan, as he prayed for us, for our family, for our new daughter, Roslyn, Delane, and me. We could feel His presence, and it was glorious, indeed!

Roslyn has lived with us now for almost ten years, and she has grown into a remarkable young lady with a love for the Lord, and a heart for all things young: babies, toddlers, and yes, any young animal, wild or domestic. She has taken on Delane's outgoing and gregarious personality, and she "has never met a stranger." Roslyn has become a part of our legacy, together with our two grown sons and our grand-children, as they will undoubtedly carry on the ministries that we've supported and served.

But a bit of background is warranted here. You see, Delane and I married in our forties, and with two sons already (my stepsons), we had no plans to have any more children. But God knew otherwise. So on another beautiful warm Monday in February 2015, one week after we had met with the MK leaders in our backyard and embarked on our new direction of starting a summer program, Delane received the call. It was from a young family friend whom we had known for several years. She was Roslyn's mom, and she had kind of adopted Delane as her surrogate mom, a role that Delane had readily accepted with love.

Roslyn's mom had had a difficult childhood with a mom addicted to drugs and a father who had other issues. As she grew up, she had gone down similar roads, turning to drugs along the way, which con-tributed to a vagabond-like lifestyle, moving from one new acquain-tance's home to another, unable to support herself or her daughter, Roslyn. Delane had tried to get her help and counseling along the way, but her efforts had failed.

So, on that Monday in February, she had called Delane as her only hope. She explained that Arizona Child Protective Services was at her current home, an apartment she shared with six others, and they were going to remove five-year-old Roslyn based on the agency's directive for protecting children. They would take her to a children's facility, where they would then attempt to place her in a foster home, unless there was a family member or friend who could take her in. And that was us, the "family friend" whom God had chosen. And that's what we did.

After three long years of numerous applications, documentation, legal proceedings, and general bureaucratic obstacles, Roslyn was ours, and we were hers. Yes, she was our "gift" from Him, and we were His "gift" to her!

Author's Note:

By the grace of God, it is with great pleasure to report that five years after Roslyn's adoption, and ten years after she came to live with us, her mother is living a new life, clean of drugs, gainfully employed, and raising three of her children whom she has had since Roslyn came to live with us.

CHAPTER 26

Wrinkles

By the end of the third year of our Mentor Kids Summer Camp, we had a smooth-running program. In addition to our backyard, we had been able to utilize two classrooms at our church (increasing to four in the following years), which was only six minutes from our home by school bus, and as mentioned, we had added a week of VBS to the kids' June activities. Yes, we were on our way, and although the program experienced a few wrinkles along the way, seven years later, we were blessed to hold our tenth annual Summer Enrichment Program with eighty-five kids in attendance, and here's what led to that.

I remember our first day as if it were yesterday. A huge, bright-orange school bus pulled up in front of our driveway in the cul-de-sac where we live. It was June first, at nine thirty a.m., on a hot, sunny day in Scottsdale, and twenty smiling, laughing elementary-aged kids got off that bus and walked and ran through the gate to the backyard. We had spent weeks spiffing up the backyard in preparation for that day. We had installed awning-covered shade areas to supplement our covered patio, under which we had set up six-foot folding tables with benches, added a buoy rope to the pool to rope off the deeper part, roped off the lawn from the pool area so the only access would be at the shallow end, repainted the playset, spread out Navajo blankets in the shady areas, and put out five-gallon plastic Gatorade watercoolers, one with water and one with lemonade.

We soon realized that spiffing up and setting up was not just a pre-program effort. You see, beginning that first year, and then every weekday in June for the next ten-plus years, we would need to set up the pool and patio in the morning before the kids arrived, then clean up the patio, pool, and lawns every afternoon after they left, followed by washing, drying, and rolling up forty to sixty towels every evening, which we put out in baskets the next morning for the kids to use.

Well, things started off somewhat chaotic as the kids ran here and there, but after a few minutes, Wendy and her crew had rounded them up, and they were ready to begin the day. After they all had eaten breakfast, they were divided into groups by age, then split up with one group of six or eight in the pool for lessons, one group on the patio for crafts, and one group on blankets in shady areas for reading and Bible study. And so it began, and shortly thereafter, we experienced our first wrinkle.

It seemed that our wooden playground—with fort, slide, picnic table, and swings, which had been installed for our grandkids a few years prior—served well for three or four youngsters, but when a group of eight or twelve of these energetic, young dynamos all got going at once, it wasn't looking good. While no one else seemed to notice, I found myself cringing as the playground would sway or the posts would rock in their insets in the ground. Clearly this would not do. But with His backing, and much to my surprise, we went out and were able to purchase a larger and much sturdier commercial set at a local playground provider. Well, I wouldn't have believed it if I hadn't seen it, but they were able to install it two days later. First wrinkle dealt with!

The second wrinkle was much more significant. You see, we live in Scottsdale, Arizona, in the Sonoran Desert, in the Phoenix metro area known as the "Valley of the Sun," one of the hottest places in the country. Over the years we had found that June was usually a relatively bearable month, temperature-wise, usually starting out with highs in the nineties and heading up to the low one hundreds by the end of the month. And that was okay. As they say, "It's a dry heat"! Fortunately, the weather did cooperate for that first year. Yes, by the end of the

God Whispers Are Life Changers

month, just as temperatures were starting to soar, our June program was ending, and things had worked out just fine.

Then came our second year, and that's when the weather stopped cooperating. By the end of the first week in June, temperatures had soared to 115 degrees, a temperature that worked well for swimming lessons, but not so much for sitting on blankets in the shade reading or studying the Bible. No, that wouldn't do. We hadn't planned for this, so we "punted." We spread out the Navajo blankets across our entire living room, family room, and dining room floors, and for thirty days, we had some forty kids sitting on floors throughout our home enjoying reading, Bible, and arts and crafts. The program had gone on, but clearly this wouldn't be a sustainable option if it was to grow in future years.

We needed air-conditioned space, and we needed classrooms, not living and family rooms. And then came His *whisper*. It pointed us to our church, which had recently embarked on a large building expansion, which had included the construction of a wonderful children's building complete with large classrooms that would each hold forty or fifty kids around eight-chair round tables, along with a large meeting hall designed for two hundred kids to attend Sunday children's services.

But there was one thing more to this *whisper*. From all those years when we had volunteered at AWANA, we had known, and fostered a great relationship with, Pastor Ryan, who ran the children's programs at our church. So we had a friend and an ally in him. To make a long story short, we called and met with Pastor Ryan to explain our plight and our program. Now, MK was not new to our church's staff and leaders, as their local outreach ministry had been providing funding assistance for MK's One-on-One Mentoring Program for years. So, they knew the ministry but not the Promise Neighborhood Program, nor the summer program we had started. With Pastor Ryan in our corner, however, and seeing that this whole summer program had been led by God all along, he ran it up the chain of command at the church, and we got our approval and our classrooms. Our Summer Enrichment Program suddenly had a future! Wow, God had provided!

MK revised the program format so the kids could be bused to the church and split into groups rotating between the classrooms, which, at that point, included STEM, in addition to Bible, reading, and arts and crafts, and each group would in turn be bused to and from our backyard for swimming, playground, and water games. So every hour and twenty minutes or so, they would rotate, and with every rotation, one group would ride the school bus to our house for swimming lessons and backyard fun, and the group that had just finished these activities would ride the bus back to the church and rotate to their respective next classroom. The entire group would stay at church all week when VBS was running and attend that incredible, God-led program along with one thousand other kids (but more on that later).

Over the past ten years, we have seen more than six hundred Palomino Promise Neighborhood kids come through the Summer Enrichment Program. They've learned about their loving God, they've learned to swim, and students' reading test scores have improved over every summer. Some of the kids who attended their first camp at the age of five or six, are now in high school and are active in MK's "i-Leader" Program, mentoring the younger kids (but more on that later). Yes, the summer program has been a resounding success and a blessing to so many children, and it all started with a *whisper* on a warm February day that had come from virtually out of nowhere. No, we hadn't planned on starting a summer camp and running it for ten years and more, and we hadn't seen it coming, but He had. He had known all along!

GOD NOTE
Disneyland at Church

It's hard for many middle-class Americans to imagine, but here's what it's like. You're a seven-year-old second-grader living in Palomino. Your parents moved to the United States from Mexico before you were born, and they still don't speak English. Together with your parents, two brothers, and a sister, you live in a small, two-bedroom trailer on a tiny lot of hard dirt with no trees and only a few shrubs here and there that have grown from seeds blown in on the wind. You live in Phoenix, Arizona, a city that averages 111 days of temperatures exceeding 100 degrees each year, but your trailer has no air-conditioning. Your parents work two jobs each and are gone much of the time. You've never been to a carnival or a water park, and Disneyland is just something you see on TV from time to time.

But this year, as part of Mentor Kid's Summer Splash Camp, you're getting to go to Vacation Bible School (VBS) at a large church in Scottsdale, Arizona, with a thousand other kids every day for a full week during the month of June, one of the hottest months of the year. Yes, to these kids, VBS is everything that Disneyland is and more, minus the rides but adding the "God" factor. Yes, that's what it's like.

Kids are greeted upon their arrival each morning at nine o'clock sharp, by two hundred staff and volunteers cheering as they enter. They're given brightly colored VBS T-shirts to wear for the week and assigned to small groups of around thirty kids for activities. The day starts in the large worship center, an amphitheater-type auditorium that holds sixteen hundred people. It has a large stage spanning the entire front of the auditorium with Jumbotron screens on both sides and a sound system that rivals any stadium rock-concert venue.

The crowd of kids is welcomed by the emcee for the week, Pastor Ryan, who leads the children's ministry at the church. As the opening event unfolds, the music is loud, the kids are laughing and screaming, and things start off with a professionally choreographed high-quality show, based on the "theme" for the year's VBS, which that year was "Galactic Starveyors," explained as follows: "Turn your telescopes to the sky and join the Galactic Starveyors, where your VBS kids will explore the vastness of space to learn about the infinite God who wants a personal relationship with them. Searching the Invisible, discovering the Invisible."

So, with music blaring, and spectacular entertainment capturing every kid's wildest imagination and interest, VBS started. The show was followed by thunderous music, with the kids singing along, complete with clapping hands and stomping feet. After the opening event, groups moved on to separate venues and activities, including games in the gym, learning sessions, Bible story reenactments, various competitions, and much, much more.

Beginning with the third year of the MK Summer Splash Camp and continuing every year thereafter, the MK kids, with a "special invitation" from the church, have attended VBS at Scottsdale Bible Church. Yes, to these Palomino kids, VBS is truly "Disneyland at church"!

Workers harvesting tilapia with nets at the
Kabwata Orphanage fish farm

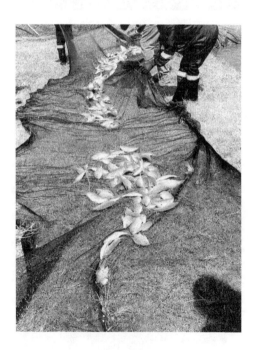

Fish farm catch

Adoption Day for Roslyn, at the Scottsdale Bible Church
Chapel for a blessing with Pastor Ryan

Angela Miyanda, former Second Lady of Zambia,
founder and "mom" of Kabwata Orphanage, shown with
author's daughter, Roslyn, and granddaughter, Haylee

God Whispers Are Life Changers

Cameroon widows meeting to discuss their microloan businesses

Christmas at Kabwata Orphanage

Christmas joy

Mentor Kids, USA (MK) Summer Splash Camp arrival by
bus on the first day of June camp

God Whispers Are Life Changers

MK group photo on first day of summer camp

MK kids starting the day at summer camp with prayer

MK kids spread out in author's home for Bible lessons during the second year of camp, when temperatures in Phoenix soared to over 100 degrees, too hot to be outdoors

MK summer camp swim lessons

MK summer camp STEM lessons

MK summer camp swim lesson certificates and medals

Kids arriving at Vacation Bible School (VBS) during summer camp

God Whispers Are Life Changers

PART IV
"For I Know the Plans"

CHAPTER 27

A New Season

In business, as in life, there are seasons. And after having parted company with our former investment partner, as well as their former director and his new company, it was time for a new season for ParaWest. Without these partners/clients, ParaWest was in need of a new investment partner if we were to continue on our path of acquiring apartment communities as well as managing them. Of course, we still had our financial partner, which would enable us to place large loans on properties that we acquired, but we needed an investor/partner capable of placing down large, multimillion-dollar blocks of equity capital.

Well, we already had the answer that would lead us into this new season and meet this need. You see, His *whisper* had planted the seed four years earlier, showing us the direction and means to move forward. And that's just what we did. By the end of the following year, we had closed on our first apartment acquisition utilizing a new source of capital. And over the course of the four years after that, we acquired and assumed the management of five additional properties, as well, and here's what led up to that.

It all originated during the Obama administration, in the aftermath of the Great Recession. In response to a decrease in small business activity in the wake of the financial crisis of 2008, Congress began developing a relief plan, which later became legislation known as the JOBS Act, which stood for "Jumpstart Our Business Startups." The law was intended to encourage the funding of small businesses by easing many of the country's securities regulations. The bill was signed into law by President Obama on April 5, 2012, and it went into effect on various dates thereafter as prescribed by the bill. Title III of the Act was known as the "CROWDFUND Act." This section created a way for companies to use "crowdfunding" to issue securities, something that was not previously permitted.

Crowdfunding is basically offering an investment opportunity to a large group (i.e., a crowd) of investors to raise capital. The new law allowed companies to raise money from small but qualified investors, with government-imposed qualifications designed to protect small investors from unscrupulous schemes. On the investment side, investment minimums as low as five thousand dollars or even less would enable tens of thousands of investors who couldn't participate in large investment-fund opportunities such as apartment properties prior to the Act, to invest in them and attain the financial benefits that had previously been available only to the wealthy. On the capital-raising side, apartment owners and others could raise capital without the previously required onerous and expensive burdens imposed by the SEC (the U.S. Securities and Exchange Commission), which had made such capital undertakings entirely prohibitive for small businesses.

So there it was. A new path for a new season. He had whispered, and we had heard. We started down this road by contacting three of the top apartment crowdfunding companies to test the waters as to their interest in our background and track record. There are different crowdfunding companies for different types of businesses, and most of them specialized in particular industries. There were several that specialized in raising money for apartment transactions, and we had selected three of the top firms. We were quite encouraged as two of them came back to us expressing their strong interest in working with us if we brought a good opportunity, a good apartment investment deal. So with that, we began our acquisition outreach to try to find a deal.

Well, the right opportunity came up shortly thereafter, a ninety-six-unit property in a suburb of Houston. Built in 1999, this was a wonderful, little apartment community in the small suburban town of Rosenburg, southwest of Houston—a perfect opportunity. We had been looking for a "smaller" property for our first crowdfunding offering to minimize our risk, in case the investment community didn't respond positively to our offering, and this ninety-six-unit property fit that bill.

So we negotiated the purchase and were able to place the property under contract. We then needed to raise the equity capital to close the deal. To do so, we went back to the two interested crowdfunding companies, approaching each of them with this outstanding investment opportunity we were pursuing. Both companies expressed an interest, so it really came down to the "terms," as to which one looked better from our perspective.

Now, crowdfunding companies are in business to make money just like everybody else. These relatively new companies had been capitalized by hefty venture capital firms, firms that invest large amounts of capital in "startup" companies with the intention of seeing high, way above-average, returns down the road, as the startups become established and grow in value.

Crowdfunding companies required a lot of capital to get started in order to hire their extensive staff and to produce their technology platforms, complex computer systems designed to reach out to potential investors, and then to manage and report to thousands of investors on up to one hundred or more investment deals as the crowdfunding company grows. So it takes a lot of capital. For their efforts, and the venture capitalist's investments, these crowdfunding companies make money through various avenues related to the investments they pursue (such as our apartment property offering), by charging fees, participating in profits, and other methods.

So part of our decision in selecting whom to work with was based on the cost of raising money through them. The other part of the decision related more to our opinion as to which one would do a better job for us, and which one would be more reputable and professional to work with. After careful consideration, we selected our crowdfunding company and went to work, preparing our presentation materials, holding a webinar, and responding to queries from potential investors, while at the same time working toward acquiring the property by placing the financing and completing all the necessary underwriting analysis, inspections, and so forth.

The response from potential investors was overwhelmingly favorable, and we raised the full equity investment capital in less than thirty days. After completing our loan processing, we were able to close on that property a month later, becoming the proud owners of our first crowdfunding transaction, a first-class apartment property in Rosenberg, Texas. Yes, His *whisper* had led to this new opportunity, an opportunity that had been born out of the depths of the Great Recession by an Act of Congress, an opportunity leading us into a new season, a season of hope and promise.

GOD NOTE
KFC and Kabwata

It was Easter morning, the last day of our second trip to visit the kids at Kabwata, and we wanted this day to be special. With Easter being such an important and highly regarded holiday in our world, we wanted to bring some of that world to the kids. Now, with Kabwata Orphanage being a Christian ministry, the children grew up knowing the Lord, attending church on Sundays, and practicing what was preached. But without the means to celebrate beyond attending worship in their local church that Easter Sunday, they hadn't planned anything more. So we planned it for them.

When we had first set our travel schedule and realized that we'd be in Lusaka on Easter Sunday, Delane and Roslyn immediately went to work. Roslyn was too young to make the trip at that time, but she relished the thought of surprising those kids on Easter Sunday, so she dove in energetically and enthusiastically. Together, they purchased candy, petite stuffed animals, small games, and other tiny toys of every type. And in the American Easter tradition, they purchased Easter baskets—in this case, small, colorful wire baskets that could be folded up to fit in a suitcase.

All of this they accumulated, enough to make seventy Easter baskets for the kids. The task was made more difficult as it all had to be compressed and stuffed into one large, hard-shelled suitcase for the nine-thousand-mile flight to take it all to the kids at Kabwata, and then re-assembled at the orphanage. But it was a task they undertook with joy in their hearts and smiles on their faces.

During the week, while we were touring Kabwata, the rural villages, and other points of interest in and around Lusaka on that trip, we formulated the next part of our plan together with the BWA folks traveling with us. While traveling about the city, we had come across just the thing. Next to the small hotel at which we were staying was none other than a KFC—Kentucky Fried Chicken—except in the local language, it was known as *Vinta Nindu Mwamba*. Well, who would have thought? We later learned that KFC had opened their first outlet in Lusaka just a few years prior. So here it was, our solution for Easter dinner!

After church that Easter morning, we arrived at Kabwata with KFC chicken and fixin's for seventy kids and ten adults, and we set up a buffet line to serve the children. We ate at picnic tables on the lawns in the courtyard of the orphanage campus, and you can bet that every "finger-lickin'" morsel of that chicken and fixin's was devoured down to the bones. But that wasn't the end of our Easter celebration that day, because after dinner, we distributed seventy brightly colored, candy- and toy-laden Easter baskets to the kids of Kabwata Orphanage. In keeping with the reason for the celebration, we had inserted into each basket a colorful Easter card we had also brought with us, a card that had the following words printed on each of them: *"Jesus said, 'I am the resurrection and the life. Whoever believes in me, though he die, yet shall he live'* (John 11: 25, ESV)," along with a "Happy Easter" note from Bread and Water for Africa.

What a wonderful gift for these kids who had never seen an Easter basket before in their young lives. Their smiles could have lit up a football stadium, but instead they lit up our hearts. Yes, His presence was palpable that day, and the joy we felt left us with memories for a lifetime.

CHAPTER 28

The Black Swan

A black swan is an unpredictable event that is beyond what is normally expected of a situation and has potentially severe consequences. Black swan events are characterized by their extreme rarity, severe impact, and the widespread insistence that they were obvious in hindsight.

Excerpted from *Investopedia*

The last two years of the second decade of the twenty-first century were good to ParaWest and to the ministries we served. ParaWest was expanding, and the children we were serving at Kabwata and Mentor Kids were growing and thriving. Over the previous two years, we had purchased four more apartment communities using our crowd-funding resources, and during the first quarter of 2020, we had two new transactions under contract to purchase and were beginning to arrange financing and prepare our offering materials for crowdfunding.

And that's when it happened—the beginning of the worst pandemic in a hundred years. It came on like a lion and had the greatest impact on the world economy seen in modern times. Yes, it was a "black swan event." No one had seen it coming, and no one could stop it. Between January 2020 and December 2021, nearly fifteen million people died worldwide due to the coronavirus disease. The pandemic brought the world economy to its knees, and its effects would impact financial markets and individuals' lives for years to come.

As the pandemic grew, community by community, country by country, it had the potential to crush ParaWest, as well as most other businesses in the United States, and, indeed, it tried. It was only by the grace of God that ParaWest made it through. While the pandemic's impact would stretch on long into the future, by the end of its first year, we were on our feet and doing business in this new COVID and post-COVID world. Yes, we were moving on, we were okay, and here's what led up to that.

The pandemic's impact on ParaWest began slowly. We had first heard of it in January 2020, when media reports came forth of a new disease, originating in China, which had horrible potential and was spreading, country by country. We didn't think much of it at first. Bread and Water for Africa had been actively working in third-world countries to prevent the spread of Ebola and other dangerous, highly contagious diseases, and governments had typically been successful in containing them.

But as media reports multiplied, along with reported cases of the disease, COVID-19, as it had been named, our business remained unaffected. That was, until March, when California became the first state to issue a "stay at home" order, requiring residents to stay home except for essential job or shopping needs. Now, California is an extremely progressive state, and they seem to go over the top on a lot of things, so at first, we weren't particularly concerned. That was, until other states started to follow suit, with Arizona following soon thereafter, followed by Texas shortly after that. It was as though a huge black curtain had descended on our world, with people suffering and dying, businesses closing, and no one knowing what would happen next, or when, if ever, this all might end.

Before the lockdowns in Arizona and Texas had even been called, we had cancelled and backed out of the purchase contracts on the two properties. The financial markets, including the crowdfunding platforms, had become volatile by mid-February, and investors were deferring investment decisions due to the uncertainty of the situation.

But that was okay since we still had all our management business, and we could start up acquisitions again after the emergency had passed.

Or so we thought. On March 10, 2020, the governor of Arizona went on television and announced the "stay at home order." It was set to last two weeks, but it would later be extended. About a week after that, Texas followed suit, and there we were. Our world had been entirely shut down. No one could work. No one would get paid. And few would be able to pay the rent on their apartments—*our* apartments. The black curtain had gotten darker and heavier in our world.

The pandemic impacted our world in so many ways—except for one. During the first and subsequent years of the pandemic, none of our employees got seriously ill; in fact, only a few ever got sick at all, but all the other impacts were dreadful. Because we were in the apartment business, providing housing to individuals and families, we were considered an "essential business," and therefore we could remain open, and our employees would continue to work. But many people were fearful of leaving their homes, fearful of this unknown, potentially fatal disease that early on, no one really knew much about.

An initial impact was the requirement for extensive cleaning and sterilization of all public places. Apartment communities have lots of those. Our employees needed to source cleaning materials and chemicals and constantly clean and disinfect. And to prevent liability exposure—that is, to prevent being sued if someone contracted COVID and said it was due to unclean surfaces at one of our apartment communities—all this needed to be logged and documented. It was an onerous task.

To complicate things further, cleaning materials were particularly sparse during the pandemic, as stores frequently ran out of supplies. Our creative people were able to find sources, however, and we were able to keep up with the need. It's notable that by the second year of the pandemic, health officials had determined that the disease was actually airborne and didn't spread by touching surfaces, which led us to realize that the early requirements for cleaning and disinfecting, while not wholly unwarranted, had apparently taken us down the wrong road along the way.

The biggest impacts of the pandemic on ParaWest were financial. Apartment residents couldn't work, and therefore, they couldn't pay their rent. As things unfolded, however, government assistance became available, and out-of-work residents could apply to numerous agencies for financial assistance, including the payment of their rent. The only problem was, these programs all had extensive and rather cumbersome application requirements, and many of our less-computer-knowledgeable residents had difficulty completing the applications. So, as things progressed and aid programs rolled out, our employees became experts in these application processes, in order to assist our residents, both to help them keep a roof over their heads and also so we could keep our income flowing in.

But rental assistance didn't reach everyone, and many apartment residents still couldn't afford their rent, either due to not meeting the qualifications for assistance, or because they were working minimal hours, or for other reasons related to the chaotic world of the pandemic. And so our apartment communities had higher and higher levels of unpaid rent (i.e., bad debt), and they began losing money after paying expenses and the mortgages. It was a scary time for apartment owners.

Even as rent collections decreased, apartment owners still had to pay their expenses and mortgage payments or face potential foreclosure. And although the media touted the federal government's program for "abating" mortgage payments for certain government-guaranteed loans (i.e., temporarily cease requiring mortgage payments to be made), the reality was that lenders attached strings—requirements that were so onerous that most owners couldn't accept them or comply. So there was no abatement for them.

Yes, things were dark, indeed. But then the federal government came up with a plan to help small businesses, including apartment properties. It was called the Payroll Protection Plan, known as "PPP," a government plan to assist small businesses with their expenses during this dark time in order to keep them afloat. And as we learned of this new program, we heard God's *whisper* that we would be okay. But the *whisper* seemed faint, and we still had our doubts and worries.

As the program rolled out in March, our revenue levels were continuing to drop, as residents had more and more difficulties paying their rent. The PPP program application process was relatively complex. It required documentation of the prior year's payroll records, as well as various other records substantiating expenses and such. The application had to go through a government-approved bank, which had to collect the application and documents and underwrite the loan in accordance with their own requirements, prior to submitting it to the federal government for final underwriting, approval, and funding.

We immediately contacted our CPA firm and enlisted their help. We also contacted our bank representatives to start the application process. And that's when the curtain darkened even more. First, our bank took weeks to initiate their own application process and make it available for customers such as us to apply. Second, the program had a finite dollar amount allocated to make the loans, and with thousands of small businesses set to apply, it was a race to make the "first come, first serve" process and hope to receive a loan allocation before the funds ran dry.

Our accounting and CPA staff worked tirelessly to compile the documentation and format the applications to the best of their ability so as not to be declined for an error or omission. And our bank representative worked closely with us to get our application into their system as it became available. So we completed our application and submitted it through our bank. Even as we did so, however, our revenues were declining each month, and we knew that ParaWest and our properties were in peril.

And then came the seemingly final blow. The federal government announced through the media and the banks that they had met their allocated funding levels, and those who had not yet been notified that they were approved would not be. The darkness darkened, and sleepless nights were the norm. But even as our faith weakened, His faithfulness never did!

Yes, approximately one month later, the federal government announced a new, larger allocation for the program, and as our application was still in the system, it would move forward accordingly. And that's exactly what it did. Two weeks later, we received an email notifying us that our PPP loan had been approved, and much to my surprise, it would be funded to our bank account the next day. Hallelujah! I remember the feeling as my heart pounded, and sitting in my office, I turned my gaze upward and whispered a "Thanks!" With the proceeds from the government-assistance loan, ParaWest and all the apartment properties we managed were able to make it through the pandemic.

Yes, the black swan event had materialized, and the dark curtain had descended on our world, but in the end, our faith had been restored, and He had led us through!

CHAPTER 29

The Wrecking Ball

"The Pandemic was a wrecking ball, and we're still tallying the damage," concluded a report from the Center of Reinventing Public Education published in *Education Weekly* two years after the pandemic had begun. It went on to say, "The Pandemic was a disaster for K-12 schools on almost all fronts, from academics to mental health to special education services. That is what we do know. But the extent of the damage is still coming into focus, and big gaps remain in our understanding of the full effect the Pandemic has had on public education."

The Palomino elementary school had been closed from March 2020 to March 2021. School was held online, but many of the kids from Palomino had no computers at home and no internet even if they had a device. Despite these challenges, however, the kids in Mentor Kids' afterschool and summer programs grew and developed during this time. They minimized the distress to their academic standings, and they participated in social activities to which few other children in Phoenix or any other city had access. Yes, MK and God's *whisper* had led them through this dark time, and here's what led up to that.

The report cited above went on to describe more of its findings. It found that "Hispanic and low-income students were disproportionately affected by schools being closed. Students in high poverty schools lost the equivalent of twenty-two weeks of instruction compared with a loss of (just) thirteen weeks in high-income schools, and income-based gaps in elementary math achievement grew by twenty percent." Additionally, "students' mental health and well-being suffered considerably as rates of anxiety and depression rose among children and adolescents."

But that's not what the Palomino kids experienced. Although they were still affected by the lockdowns and school closures, the Palomino kids were spared the worst of it. To some measure, it was like the Old Testament story of the Passover, in which the "angel of death" passed over God's chosen ones and the plague didn't affect them the way it affected everyone else. During the pandemic, with Mentor Kids' programs, leaders, and volunteers shepherding these kids through the lockdowns, the closed schools, the online learning, and the chaos of it all, they were protected from the worst effects of the pandemic—from the "wrecking ball."

It started in March 2020, when the "stay at home" (i.e., "lockdown") order initially took effect and schools were closed. During the early weeks of the "lockdown," there could be little direct contact with the kids, so MK staff initiated contact through Facebook and Teams, an online meeting app, to stay in touch. MK staff would also drop off "activity packets" to the children's homes, as well as food boxes for those who needed such assistance. By June of that year, "contact" was again allowed, and MK held the Summer Enrichment Program as it had been doing for years, but with a few adjustments. The first adjustment was related to the classrooms. Our church was still closed, but Rivers Church, located near Palomino, made their classrooms available to MK.

We held the swim program at our house as always, and we bused the kids from the new church location, where they would have classroom sessions on Bible study and reading. The program was a scaled-down version of what we had done in previous years, with enrollment also down—only around forty-five kids attending instead of the previous year's sixty-five. Many of the kids wore protective masks, but it wasn't required. For the kids who did attend, it was a wonderful month. Not only did they benefit from the summer reading, but they were able to get out of their homes and have some fun. As some of the kids attending that year shared with us, they had not been anywhere outside their homes for more than three months prior to summer camp.

With schools still closed in August, when the next school year began, MK ran a full-day program for the Palomino kids at a nearby campus of our church that had reopened. The program initially ran from 8 a.m. to 2 p.m., with MK shortly thereafter adding an afternoon program from 2:30 to 5 p.m. The morning session had the kids in computer labs working on their online school assignments using computers provided by MK. Afternoon sessions would include tutoring students as needed, as well as providing reading classes and playground activities. These programs went on for nearly a year until schools reopened and kids could return. As an added blessing, the school our daughter, Roslyn, attended had opened by the fall of 2021, and she and some of her middle-school friends took the opportunity to volunteer at the MK afternoon sessions that year, helping out. Roslyn's love for little kids brought her tons of joy and endeared her to the children as she helped with reading and led games on the playground.

By the fall of 2021, things were getting back to normal "somewhat," and Palomino Elementary School, along with many others, reopened. Students returned, and despite some of the unusual safety precautions that remained in effect, life for the Palomino kids and other students across the country pretty much returned to normal. And although the Palomino kids had been spared the worst of the damaging effects, many others hadn't. Many kids returning to school after that year of lockdowns and online schooling were way behind in their learning, behind in their social skills, and behind in their overall development, and it would take years to catch up.

Yes, the pandemic had, indeed, been a "wrecking ball" for America's schoolchildren, and it had only been by God's grace, activated through Mentor Kids USA, that the kids from Palomino had been protected and shepherded through it.

GOD NOTE
The Gideons

"In the fall of 1898, two traveling men, strangers to each other, met in a Wisconsin, U.S.A. hotel. Discovering each other to be a Christian, they held their evening devotions together. The Lord impressed upon them the idea of forming an association." Their objective was to "seek to spread the Bible, the Word of God, and to encourage its use as widely as possible." To accomplish this objective, the Gideons would place Bibles in rooms in hotels and other public places, including hospitals and prisons. Over the next 120-plus years, the Gideons placed Bibles in hotels and other locations in over 170 countries. The program is nonsectarian and supported by thousands of evangelical churches worldwide.

— Excerpted from the Gideon Bible

During the early growth years of ParaWest, Delane and I spent many nights in hotels in Texas and California as we expanded into those markets. We often traveled individually to cover the different territories, with Delane covering California and me covering Texas. During those travels, and many lonely nights in hotel rooms, we each individually heard His whisper as we first noticed the Gideon Bibles placed in the rooms, and we first read their story, printed in the front pages of their Bibles. Yes, it was their story, and their Bibles, that inspired us to start our own Bible distribution outreach.

Now, we never intended for our distribution to be anything along the lines of the Gideons, but we did decide that the children, individuals, and families we served, should have access to the Word of God, and thus our own humble distribution program began. We started with the classrooms for the MK after-school program. We had observed at our own church while serving in AWANA that every elementary classroom had a shelf of children's Bibles—colorful story Bibles with pictures throughout to engage young students in their learning. So we provided similar storybook Bibles for the classrooms of the elementary students in the Palomino after-school program.

Next, we distributed Bibles to the kids living at the Kabwata Orphanage in Africa. Because these students varied from early elementary all the way through high school, we sent different Bibles for different age groups. They ranged from picture Bibles for the youngest kids, to early reading editions for those just learning to read, and teen Bibles for the older, middle-school and high-school kids.

Our next foray into Bible distribution was to the ladies in Cameroon, to whom we distributed Bibles written in French, the primary language spoken there.

Our largest distribution to date was made at the first fall festival we held at Palomino Park (but more on that later), where we distributed more than two hundred Spanish and English Bibles to parents and individuals who lived in Palomino.

As the Gideons proclaimed, "God has promised to bless His Word and to cause it to bear fruit that will honor Him."

With that we agree, and because of God's *whisper* many years ago in those lonely hotel rooms in Houston and San Jose, California, a few more children and families in a low-income neighborhood in Phoenix, Arizona, as well as orphans in Zambia, and widowed women in Cameroon, are blessed to have "His Word" in their own hands.

CHAPTER 30
A Brighter Day

So there we were, in the last week of January, two years after the pandemic, at the world-class Las Ventana's Al Paraiso Resort, in sun-drenched Cabo San Lucas on the Sea of Cortez, celebrating our twentieth year in business. We were at our first-ever executive retreat, along with a dozen of our senior management personnel and their spouses/significant others. The retreat was sponsored by Delane and me, and it had been planned for our twentieth year of business as a reward for our senior management team, who had worked so hard over the years to help our business grow and succeed.

It was also an appropriate reward for a team that, two years prior, when the worldwide pandemic struck, had buckled down and worked unceasingly to help us get through a very rocky and difficult time, a time when so many other businesses failed, including many in our industry. Most of all, though, the retreat was a way to share God's blessings, which have been great indeed, and here's what led up to that.

For more than a year, the pandemic had pummeled our business. The world was trying to move on, but the impacts of the pandemic kept pulling us backward. Small businesses continued to suffer throughout the United States as lockdowns and limited openings caused many to fail, and many apartment residents lost jobs, suffering severe financial setbacks as a result.

Our apartment staffs did double duty during that time, fulfilling their normal duties and then working with residents to help them obtain "rental assistance" through the various programs that government agencies had rolled out. Our accounting staff had the tacked-on responsibility of managing the Payroll Protection Program, which had onerous reporting requirements in order to utilize the program's funding to supplement lower rental collections being realized at the apartment properties. Many of our employees were also fearful of coming to work and exposing themselves to the dreaded COVID disease, and we enacted policies to allow those who worried or were most vulnerable to work from home.

Despite everyone's exemplary efforts, though, business was difficult that first year of the pandemic. Morale was low, and it was hard for anyone to see the "light at the end of the tunnel." Day after day, the media would show discouraging pictures, events, and stories of the horrors and "potential horrors" of the pandemic.

By the end of the first year, things began to return to some semblance of "normalcy." Most schools had reopened, as had most businesses previously subjected to lockdowns, and our employees, along with many of our renters, were enjoying a return to normal in their lives. It wasn't as though the world had become brighter, but it was a little less dark than it had been for quite some time. And people took comfort in that.

As we moved further into the second year following the start of the pandemic, ParaWest's opportunities returned, referrals for management accounts kept us busy, and we restarted our acquisition business, closing on our next crowdfunded apartment acquisition before the end of the year. Yes, the sky was indeed opening, and it was a brighter day.

So, as the year went on, it occurred to us that the following year was our "twentieth year" in business, a milestone, and something that should be recognized. And that's when the thought hit us—we should hold a retreat in celebration. Now, with the pandemic recently at our heels, we wouldn't be able to undertake a full employee retreat, but we could reward those senior executives who had been with us for many, many years and whose hard work and determined efforts had led us through the dark days of the pandemic. And that's just what we did. We planned our retreat, and in January of the following year, we were there, at the world-class Las Ventana's Al Paraiso Resort in sun-drenched Cabo San Lucas on the Sea of Cortez, celebrating our twentieth year in business.

Our retreat included plenty of fun in the sun, along with opportunities for personal development and growth. The planned activities were incredible, and included, among others:

- A day of personality assessment and training, led by Betsy Allen-Manning, a nationally known leadership speaker and bestselling author
- Team-building exercises (via *Wheel of Fortune* games)
- A catamaran sail charter, highlighted by whale-watching as humpback whales would breach the waves in front of us
- Dinner on a 110-foot yacht, motoring around the Arch of Cabo, a famous rock formation rising out of the ocean off the southern tip of the Baja Peninsula
- Entertainment by Christian comedian Stacy Pederson, capping the week off at our private dinner on the beach planned for our final evening, under a sky full of sparkling stars!

It was a wonderful week and one that will be not soon be forgotten by those who attended. Yes, the retreat was truly a way of sharing God's blessings and His deliverance through a dark and difficult time. Those blessings had been great, indeed!

GOD NOTE

In Sunshine
and in Sorrow

In Africa, as elsewhere, everything changes. But in many third-world countries, including those in Africa, civil wars, coups, government corruption, and other divisive and destructive forces seem to occur more often than in other areas around the world. As a result, people suffer, and lives are lost, often as a result of meaningless and ultimately futile uprisings or causes.

Such was the case in Bangolan Cameroon, a village in which the BWA microloan program had been rolled out and was working wonders for the villagers who had stepped up to participate. The uprising started a few years after BWA's microloan program had brought sunshine into the lives of widows in that village in northwest Cameroon. Following the dethronement of the leader of the village of Bangolan, villagers rioted, and the area was flooded with troops from the government's "Rapid Intervention Battalion" (i.e., BIR).

BIR troops were reported by the Cameroon News Agency to have committed numerous atrocities in Bangolan at the time. Many villagers were killed, and many others fled. During the years prior to and following Bangolan's crisis described here, the BIR had been exposed by Amnesty International of atrocities and war crimes throughout the country, including crimes of murder and rape, as well as illegal detention and torture.

In the village of Bangolan, homes and businesses were burnt to the ground, and villagers "were brutally beaten and butchered," as reported by Hope House, a ministry partner that had worked with Bread and Water for Africa for the previous twelve years. Included among the homes burnt were three that belonged to widows who had participated in the microloan program for the past few years. Yes, these women and many of the other villagers had become refugees themselves, as they left their homes and fled, seeking safety.

It was a time of great sorrow for those at Hope House, BWA, and Delane and me, as we read the reports from Hope House in Cameroon. To us and most Americans, whose worst slight from another might be getting cut off on the freeway or ignored by a clerk at a local store, it's hard to imagine what it is like to be subjected to such atrocities, such barbarities, to have our loved ones and neighbors, our homes and our livelihoods, ripped from us.

But such is the way in this fallen world, and to some extent, such is the way in Africa. Yet while we grieve these losses, we are comforted knowing He will give "strength to the weary" and "comfort to those who mourn," and together, we will persevere, as His blessings brighten the world for many, and so we will turn the page and go on.

CHAPTER 31

The Only Constant

When you're finished changing, you're finished.
—Benjamin Franklin

It may be true that the only thing that is constant is change.

Sears and Roebuck was one of the most iconic retail businesses of the past two hundred years. Founded in 1893 as a mail-order company, its catalogs sold everything from socks to tires to prefabricated homes, some of which are still standing today. At one time, the company had diversified into owning a credit card company and an insurance company, and it was headquartered in the tallest building in the world, the Sears Tower in Chicago. It expanded and adapted in many ways, but in the end, it failed to adapt to the changing world of ecommerce, and with the rise of Amazon and online retailing, it was eventually pushed aside and forced to file for bankruptcy in 2018.

Kodak began as a partnership between George Eastman and Henry Strong in 1892, with its release of the first Kodak camera, a "film roll camera." During most of the twentieth century, Kodak held a dominant position in the photo industry and benefited from many technological improvements along the way. Creating a new age for photography, an employee of Kodak invented the digital camera in 1975. As digital cameras became commonplace, however, and with the seismic impact that iPhones would soon have, Kodak failed to adapt and lost market share, eventually filing for bankruptcy in 2012.

Change affects everyone and everything, including businesses. ParaWest, like many other businesses, has been through a myriad of changes since its inception, and it has reinvented itself many times to get to where it is today. Through the years, we have heard His *whisper*, and we have responded. If we hadn't, ParaWest likely would have gone the way of so many other businesses in the past, and it would remain only as a memory, possibly a page in Wikipedia.

Changes taking place through the years have included technology, which has enhanced efficiency and financial performance, expanded services to clients and apartment residents, and moved into markets we had never planned on reaching. But it didn't start out this way, and here's what led us to this.

When ParaWest first started, we had no website, and the internet was still expanding, used primarily for information and communication. Ecommerce had yet to dominate the sales markets, and social media was barely beginning. So, in short, it was a much more personally interactive world, with business contacts and relationships developed through phone conversations and in-person meetings. "Snail mail" was still the dominant means of sending correspondence, although fax machines were in broad use. And that's where we started.

To reach potential clients (i.e., apartment owners), we would seek referrals from professionals in our industry, including those in banking, real estate and mortgage brokerage, and others. Additionally, we would reach out to owners by sending unsolicited correspondence, touting our successes in "turning around" apartment properties, increasing revenue, and so forth.

It was a tedious process, as well as a low-percentage game, in which probably one out of fifty contacts would actually get us in front of a potential new client to tell our story. Then it would take several such meetings to progress to a point where the potential client had the confidence in us to make the change and retain us to manage their property. These were big decisions, and successful investors and owners don't make big decisions on a whim.

Fast-forward twenty years, however, and it would be a different story. Potential clients now come to us almost exclusively from referrals by brokers, lenders, satisfied clients who have worked with us, and other property owners who know of our track record and reputation for getting results. They learn about our company, track record, performance, and services through our company website, which generates more than eight thousand hits each year and disseminates ten times the information included in our original brochure/résumé in 2003. And here's how the change has happened.

Early on, as ParaWest extended its market outreach, we moved into Houston and Dallas, Texas, and then into central coastal California, all at the request of existing clients. These new markets provided growth opportunities that the smaller markets of Phoenix and Tucson could never approach.

We upgraded our use of technology, installing the most advanced apartment management, accounting, and communication systems available, and we have recently incorporated AI into our toolbox.

We expanded our services to include property renovations, an area of opportunity that would significantly add to our revenues in subsequent years.

We moved into syndication—that is, acquiring properties and offering investor opportunities to large apartment funds as well as individuals through crowdfunding.

And most recently, ParaWest expanded into new markets from our Houston operating base, including Oklahoma, Kansas, and Tennessee, all at the request of existing clients.

Yes, change is, indeed, the only constant in this world, and only by embracing it can any business avoid becoming a history page in Wikipedia.

CHAPTER 32

Fifteen Thousand Easter Eggs

The numbers alone were staggering in our world: 15,700 candy-filled, plastic Easter eggs; 800 breakfast burritos; 2,000 bottles of water; 150 folding tables with tablecloths and centerpieces; 350 folding chairs; two church worship bands; ten inflatable bounce houses and obstacle courses; a face-painting table; twelve local ministry and service tables; one truckload of distributable groceries; one fire engine on display, accompanied by a team of firefighters; one SWAT mobile unit on display, accompanied by a SWAT captain and a half-dozen Phoenix policemen and women; 300 adult attendees; 120 volunteers; five participating churches; and 800 laughing, screaming, running, joyous toddler and elementary-aged kids, all gathered at Palomino Park on the Saturday before Easter! It was amazing—and here's what led up to that.

It was the year after the pandemic. Delane and I, along with MK's Palomino Promise Neighborhood director and our church's Hispanic ministries pastor, had gotten together for lunch to hash over a new idea. The Palomino after-school and summer programs had been so successful that we decided we wanted to "do more." God had whispered, and we wanted to reach out to their families and others in Palomino and touch their lives with our ministry. We wanted to "transform" this neighborhood for the better and have an impact on its future generations.

So, in addition to impacting the kids' lives as MK had been doing for nearly a decade, we decided to reach further out. We would hold a festival and invite the entire neighborhood. We'd serve free food and offer games for the kids, Christian music for entertainment, a message from our pastor, Bibles for everyone, Bible story coloring books for the kids, and plenty of wonderful fellowship all around. And so it began.

We started our planning, and of course, one of the first decisions to be made was location—where to hold the festival. Well, our church had a smaller, secondary campus about two miles from Palomino, and that's where our Hispanic ministries' pastor served, so it seemed kind of a natural fit. The only thing was, the campus was being expanded, and the new buildings, courtyards, and parking lots were all under construction.

We were meeting at the end of the summer and planning the fall festival for November just before Thanksgiving. We learned from church officials that the campus was scheduled for completion just a few weeks before our planned festival, so that would work. Or would it? We also learned that the construction schedule had already seen numerous delays, and no one could ensure that the campus would be completed and available by our date.

And that's when He stepped in. You see, since the church campus wouldn't be available, we had to find an alternate location, and after much consternation, we decided to take it to Palomino Park, which was located adjacent to the Palomino elementary and middle schools, in the heart of Palomino. The logistics of putting on the festival in the park would be more difficult than holding it at the church campus, but at the end of the day, it would bring our ministry into the heart of the neighborhood, which would be far more impactful than transporting neighborhood residents to the church. So now everyone could come. And everyone did.

That first fall festival was a booming success. We had five hundred attendees; we served grilled burgers and hot dogs; we had bounce houses, games, and face painting for the kids; and one hundred volunteers signed up and came out to help, along with others from the two churches who worked to put on the festival. It was a bright and warm Saturday in November, and by ten o'clock that morning, parents and kids were streaming in, walking to the park from the neighborhood as burgers sizzled on the grill and tables adorned with fall-colored cloths and centerpieces greeted them as they did. God had smiled on us that day at our first Palomino festival, but it wouldn't be the last time.

With the rousing success of that first festival, we began holding both fall and Easter festivals at the park over the ensuing years. With each new festival, we became more efficient in our planning and more expansive in our reach. By the time we held the Easter festival a few years later, we were on a roll. But even though our planning pointed us to an expanded event, including ten thousand Easter eggs, more food, more games, and more entertainment, we never dreamed the festival would grow to the extent that it did, or that participation by the churches, the volunteers, the ministries and agencies, the first responders, and others would be so extraordinarily high, along with the energy and the love to serve those kids and their families on that Saturday in April.

But turn out they did! It was a beautiful April day in Phoenix, 68 degrees when we started setup and in the low seventies as the festival geared up, with the sun shining and not a cloud in the sky. Leaders in their bright blue and volunteers in their bright orange T-shirts, custom-designed for that Easter celebration, began work at eight that morning setting up tables and chairs, the food service area, and celebratory "Welcome" and "Resurrection" banners.

Police and fire department officials arrived and set up the fire engine and SWAT mobile unit for touring (always a major hit). Colorful inflatables, ranging in size from a small toddlers' "barnyard" bounce house to an 85-foot-long, monster obstacle course with all shapes and sizes in between were lined up along the entire south side of the park. And the star of the day, the Easter eggs, of all colors of the rainbow—red, yellow, blue, green, pink, purple, orange, and more— were spread out on the two-acre lawn for the huge Easter egg hunt that was scheduled for noon.

Palomino Park consists of about four acres in total, with about half of that on the south side and half on the north. It had playgrounds, basketball courts, and walkways separating the two areas. Our group set up the festival on the south side and dispersed the Easter eggs on the north. On the south half, inflatable bounce houses, obstacle courses, and games were set up around the perimeter, with food service across from that, music consisting of worship bands with a thunderous PA system next to the inflatables, and tables and chairs throughout the middle courtyard. The entire north side of the park, which consisted of one giant lawn area, served for the Easter egg hunt.

Now, to give credit where credit is due, the entire Easter egg hunt was hosted and run by Rivers Church, the same church that offered space to the MK afterschool program during the pandemic. All eggs were donated by church members and came pre-filled when donated. Their original goal was ten thousand eggs, a challenging number we had all felt at the time. But by the time the big day had arrived, they had accumulated 15,700 eggs—a truly whopping number! The eggs were spread out on the lawn, which was divided into sections, separating toddlers, elementary-age kids, and older, to give everyone a chance. The entire lawn was roped off around the edges to prevent pre–egg hunt spoilers from jumping the gun.

So, at ten o'clock sharp, the festival began. Attendees had been streaming into the park for about a half hour, but by ten, they were coming in hoards—families, friends, kids, grandparents—it was amazing. The inflatables, games, and face painting were open upon arrival, and the first band was playing a Toby Mac song as they opened the festival. It was truly a festive atmosphere. Burritos and drinks were served at eleven, and while the crowd was enjoying the feast, an Easter message was provided by one of the pastors from a supporting church that had helped plan the festival. The message was uplifting and encouraging, and the mostly Hispanic crowd seemed to be drawn to the pastor's words.

And then it was time! Shortly before noon, someone let out a false "it's started" yell, and dozens of kids rushed the lawn area where the eggs were waiting. Several leaders and volunteers headed them off, however, and were able to contain the enthusiasm until the actual start at noon.

The hunt started with the toddlers. Little guys and gals, along with their parents, were allowed to enter the lawn area and began picking up and bagging eggs as fast as their little legs could take them. Shortly thereafter, the elementary school–age kids were released, and it became more chaotic as they ran and grabbed, and finally, as everyone else was allowed onto the lawn, full-blown calamity ensued. Everyone was respectful, however, and there were no untoward incidents; within the next ten minutes, it was all over. Eggs were in bags. Candy-wrapper remnants were all that was left on the lawn, and it was time for us, the leaders and volunteers, to clean up.

The festival had come to an end. It had been glorious, and a true blessing that day for more than one thousand attendees and volunteers. It turned out to be more than we expected, and His hand was all over it as the day unfolded. And all because of a quiet *whisper* that had asked us to "do more."

CHAPTER 33

The Next Generation

At twenty-three, Mumba, who had grown up at Kabwata Orphanage and Transit Centre, graduated from Mwanawasa Medical University in Lusaka, Zambia, having earned his medical degree in environmental health sciences. "It has been an awesome experience for me at school," he exclaimed upon his graduation. Today, Mumba is an environmental health technologist employed at a hospital in their public health department, working to prevent diseases and promote health in his home country of Zambia.

Mumba had been born to a mother in a Zambian prison who had committed atrocious crimes, and his relatives, not wanting anything to do with him because of his mother's stigma, left him with the government, which, in turn, took him to Kabwata Orphanage. There he found his new family and the loving arms of Kabwata's founder and director, Angela Miyanda. And there he grew up and became the young man he is today, with a future of hope and a love for those less fortunate, including his brothers and sisters at Kabwata.

At seventeen, Zithlali is an assistant teacher at Mentor Kids Palomino Promise Neighborhood. Additionally, she is a fledgling entrepreneur and has started her own business selling Chamoy candy—a spicy, sweet, and tangy candy popular in Mexico, and in demand in her north Phoenix neighborhood. As for her future, she plans on attending college and aspires to become either a lawyer or a criminal investigator.

Zithiali grew up in Palomino and was the oldest of three children. Her parents worked long hours, her dad working until eight each evening and her mom till eleven. So, by the age of seven, Zithiali was in charge of taking care of her younger siblings after school and into the evenings. "I feel like I didn't have a childhood," she told us at an i-Lead session. As her siblings got a little older, she joined MK's after-school program and found her new home. She quickly connected with her teachers at MK as "they were always interested in her family" and "would help her with anything she was going through."

In middle school, Zithiali advanced to MK's i-Lead Program. This program for older students helps prepare them for adulthood and their future, encompassing such areas as career planning, leadership skills, goal-setting, personal financial skills, and other areas that will help them succeed in the adult world. The iLeaders also act as mentors to the younger kids attending MK's afterschool program.

Today Zithiali has a bright future, a desire to give her siblings a "great childhood," and a heart for all the younger kids who are a part of MK. Through Zithlali's encouragement, her mom now attends church with her, and in Zithlali's words, "we are all much more thankful for what God has provided for us."

These are just two of the many success stories of children who started life in disadvantaged neighborhoods or circumstances, and through God-led assistance from loving caregivers, teachers, and volunteers, will be a part of the next generation who will have greater opportunities, greater successes, and greater self-fulfillment than the generation who went before them. That future, however, has never been a given, and it should never be taken for granted. It is the result of the focused efforts, dedication, and hard work of so many who serve each and every day to give these kids a future, and here's what led to that.

Kabwata Orphanage and Transit Centre began as a "waystation," a home to take in orphaned children until an appropriate "foster home" could be found. However, Kabwata's founder, Angela, soon found that Zambia has no viable "foster home" network, and so the children ultimately had nowhere else to go. Because of this, she established and developed the permanent orphanage. Over time, her facility grew, and more and more kids came to call Kabwata home. Kabwata not only provided a loving and nurturing environment, but Angela and her "aunties" enrolled the children in school, helped them become active in church, and shepherded them to develop and learn as they grew.

Through the years, as each of the children grew up, Angela expanded her efforts to help the now–young adults find their futures. Some went to trade schools or obtained employment; others, such as Mumba, enrolled in a university and obtained further education. More than 550 children have lived at Kabwata over the past twenty-something years, and over that time, many have grown up and gone on to productive, self-fulfilling adult lives.

Mentor Kids USA started as a one-on-one mentoring program for disadvantaged children, and it later changed direction to "adopt" Promise Neighborhoods, impoverished neighborhoods whose children need a leg up to have a better life. After running their afterschool and summer programs for several years, MK started their "i-Lead" program, for young adults in middle school through high school that provides life skills, career-development training, part-time employment, and a leg up to gain further education or skills in order to secure employment, a career, and a future.

This is our purpose—to give these kids a better future than they otherwise might have had, to introduce them to a wonderful and gracious God who will give them purpose and joy along the way, and who will be with them in good times and in bad. Yes, the next generation is truly on its way, and with God's grace, they will have better lives and leave this world a better place than where they started.

CHAPTER 34

Passing the Torch

Lit in accordance with ancient traditions by the rays of the sun in Olympia, Greece, the Olympic flame arrived in France after crossing the Mediterranean Sea. The torch symbolizes the light of spirit, knowledge and life. The torch that came all the way from Greece will be passed from the games of Paris to the games of another city four years later, symbolically indicating that the current games are connected with both past and future.

— adapted from "The Paris 2024 Games Torch,"
International Olympic Committee

As with the Olympic Games, ParaWest, too, is "passing the torch." Now, Delane and I aren't going anywhere anytime soon, and we will continue to provide the benefit of our years of experience as needed, but with the appointment of Kim and Chris as managing partners, the torch goes with them. The ParaWest of the past twenty years will be a part of, but no doubt different from, the ParaWest of the future. That ParaWest will be what Kim, Chris, and a host of others make it.

Hopefully, it will be an even better version, a "ParaWest 2.0," if you will. And hopefully that version will soar to heights unforeseen by Delane and me when we started back in 2003. And in that future version, we hope its resources will be used purposefully and prudently for God's purposes in places both at home and abroad for the betterment of mankind. Yes, that is ParaWest's future, and that is our hope, but it wasn't always so, and here's what led to that.

As we founded ParaWest back in 2003, Delane and I had no idea we were starting an entrepreneurial and ministry-driven adventure. We had no idea it would take us from our home in Scottsdale, Arizona, to so many places and purposes at home, across the country, and well beyond our borders. We had no idea of the people we would meet or the lives that would be touched. No, we were just putting one foot in front of the other and stepping out in faith.

But God, in all His wonder, had another plan. He would take us out of our neighborhood and into poorer ones. He would lead us in business to California, Texas, Oklahoma, Tennessee, and beyond, despite our original plan to keep our company "simple and small." He would take us to dusty, rural villages in Africa, in countries like Zambia and Cameroon.

He would show us His glory on the banks of the Zambezi River and at the foot of the thundering Victoria Falls. He would introduce us to ministry leaders, workers, and volunteers who gave their hearts and lives to their work helping others. And He would take us to the children, to the orphans, to the widows, to the homeless, and to the refugees, and He would give us friendships and a love for all whom we met and served along the way. Yes, it was a wonderful plan!

And so, we end as we began, by offering a prayer for you, dear reader. Our prayer is that through these pages of our God-led adventure, you may have heard some God *whispers* of your own, and that you'll find your own passion and your own self-fulfillment through a God-led adventure that will bring you all that your heart desires as you look to Him and help others along the way. God bless you!

EPILOGUE

It had been a great day on the Zambezi River. We had eluded the giant attacking crocodile, evaded the wallowing hippos, and seen God's glory in the form of majestic elephants as they drank and grazed. Back on shore that afternoon, we saw other amazing sights, including two towering giraffes and one rampaging ostrich named Oscar.

Afterward, we had dinner on the banks of the Zambezi with our BWA friends and relived the events of that day and others we had spent at Kabwata and its surrounding villages on past visits. It was a remarkable day, a glorious day. And as we dined at our long, wooden table on that remote river with the sun going down and a glowing orange sky above, we were engulfed with a sense of peace, God's peace, a wonderful feeling in this fast-paced, chaotic world in which we live.

Later that evening, as Delane and I retired to our safari lodge, we were equally spellbound with the view before us. The entire front of our room was open to the river as one large window, but it had no glass, no screens, and only a canvas cloth that was tied back until we closed it later to keep out the sun at daybreak.

As we lay there in our bed, gazing out that open window, we watched as the last light of dusk illuminated two lonely fishermen paddling by in a wooden canoe. And soon thereafter, the heavens opened up in all their glory, and the sparkles of a million stars appeared out our window, dazzling us with their brilliance. It was an incredible end to an incredible day, and we closed our eyes and whispered a soft prayer, thanking Him for blessing us so!

POSTSCRIPT I

Trilogy Publishing— TBN

So, one last "God Note." I had finished writing this book, and I was seeking an agent or a publisher to have it published and distributed. As a first-time book author, the process was new to me, but I've had a lot of experience in seeking out partners for other purposes throughout my career. So I reached out to numerous potential agents and publishers in my quest. I had gotten some initial interest, but nothing that really motivated me and said, "This is the way to go."

And then it happened. I somehow landed on the web page of Trilogy Publishing, a "wholly owned subsidiary of TBN." I don't recall how I had come across it, but as I did, I heard His *whisper* once more. Yes, this was the partner I needed. As a Christian organization, they fit the bill, and with their national and global outreach through their TV stations, they had a platform second to none. Yes, this was my direction. But… would they accept my manuscript and work with me?

My first contact with them was encouraging as we spoke about my background and my manuscript. They asked me to send a full copy for them to read and review. And so I did. And not too long after, I heard back from them. Trilogy-TBN had approved my manuscript for publication! So here we are, proving once again that while I didn't know it along the way, He had a plan all along!

POSTSCRIPT II

The following devotional (on the following page) was first published while we were finalizing this book for editing. Its message on ministry service seemed to be so closely aligned with the message of this book that we elected to include it here, with permission.

The Power in Hearing Hearts

"For this is the message you heard from the beginning: We should love one another."

– 1 John 3:11

Maybe you have a heart for ministry, and you know that God has called you to carry out big things for His Kingdom, but you feel stuck. If that's you, remember that *where you are is loaded with potential*! Unfortunately, we live in a culture where "big" wins the prize. Churches and leaders are recognized by their size and number of followers, and people mistakenly believe that influence is cultivated in quantity.

However, I want to remind you that ministry is equally impactful whether it's carried out on a large scale or in simple conversations with friends and neighbors. The key to effecting change is to care for the hearts of others. It's not about swaying opinions or making sure that large numbers of people hear your message, it's about ensuring that God's love makes a lasting imprint on precious souls. In fact, the most deeply rooted change happens through meaningful discourse that is characterized by compassion and connection and can take place anywhere.

My friend, you are called to make a difference in this world. Though your territory may not be as large as you would like it to be, your influence isn't measured by quantity or notoriety but rather by your *faithfulness*. Right under your feet, there are treasures of impact just waiting to be unearthed—you need only to use the gifts and passions already in your possession. Within you lives the same power that raised Jesus from the dead, and He has anointed you to make a difference in the lives of those around you through the powerful act of *hearing their hearts*. Your mission field is full of Kingdom blessings, and your ministry will have an eternal impact when you resolve to show God's boundless and undiscriminating love to all who are within your reach.

(Reprinted with permission from Hour of Power and Pastor Bobby Schuller, originally printed in Positive Minute Daily Devotionals, September 26, 2024)

Kabwata Orphanage Easter baskets being assembled by
Bread and Water for Africa friends

Joyful Easter basket recipient

Kentucky Fried Chicken in Zambian dialect

Kids at Kabwata lined up for a KFC buffet on Easter

God Whispers Are Life Changers

Bread and Water folks serving KFC

Cameroon microloan participant with her new Bible

Kabwata kids showing off their new Bibles

ParaWest twentieth-anniversary retreat banner

Retreat dinner fare at final night, "Dinner on the Beach," in Cabo San Lucas, Mexico

Fifteen thousand eggs at Easter egg hunt in Palomino Park

Girls having fun at the Easter festival at Palomino Park

Easter festival food stacked up and ready to serve

God Whispers Are Life Changers

Food served by church volunteers

Inflatable obstacle course, one of a dozen inflatables at the festival

Festival music, courtesy of church worship team musicians

Police SWAT mobile unit at the festival with smiling kids
poking out the top

Lonely fishermen in a wooden canoe on the Zambezi River
at dusk

Michael Salkeld

ABOUT THE AUTHOR
(AND WIFE)

Business

Together as partners in business and marriage, Michael and Delane co-founded their apartment management and investment company, ParaWest Management, in 2003 after both had led successful careers for more than twenty years. Today, with offices in Scottsdale, Arizona, and Houston, Texas, and more than two hundred employees, ParaWest has grown to be a "best in class," regional leader in the industry, currently managing a portfolio of apartment investment properties valued in excess of a half billion dollars, with locations in more than fifteen cities and five states.

Ministry Service

Michael and Delane began their first ministry service shortly after their marriage but accelerated their outreach after founding ParaWest, and that's when the real adventure began. Since 2007, they have worked with and supported ministries that serve orphans, widows, and rural villagers in Zambia, Sierra Leone, and Cameroon, Africa, and for the past ten years, they have hosted a summer camp for disadvantaged children at their home in Scottsdale, Arizona.

Family and Home

Michael and Delane have two adult children (Michael's stepsons), an adopted teenage daughter, six grandchildren, an enormous extended family of nieces, nephews, cousins, and more… and their two puppies, (brother and sister) Maltese–Shih Tzus George and Gracie.

With family spread out geographically, Michael and Delane are blessed to be able to get together with many of them on extended-family summer and Christmas vacations, often in beautiful and God whisper–inspired locations!

As longtime members of Scottsdale Bible Church, which they call "home," Michael and Delane have been active in various ministries and outreach programs over many years.

Michael and Delane were married in a simple service on a beautiful, warm, sunny day in a garden patio overlooking the Pacific Ocean at the Hotel Del Coronado, in San Diego, and recently returned there to celebrate their twenty-seventh wedding anniversary!

ENDNOTES

1   See https://archive.starbucks.com/record/our-founders.

2   See Kim Bhasin, "Gigantic Companies That Started from Nothing," *Huffington Post*, August 8, 2023.

3   See https://news.microsoft.com/announcement/ microsoft-is-born.